Decorative Painting

GARDEN GLORIES:
Painting Fruit, Vegetables & Berries
IN ACRYLIC

GARDEN GLORIES:
Painting Fruit, Vegetables & Berries
IN ACRYLIC

Prudy Vannier, CDA

NORTH LIGHT BOOKS
CINCINNATI, OHIO

Dedication

This book is dedicated to learning artists everywhere.
Keep learning and keep creating. You make the world a more
beautiful and more meaningful place to live!

03 02 01 00 99   5 4 3 2 1

Library of Congress Cataloging-in-Publication Data

Vannier, Prudy
   Garden glories : painting fruit, vegetables & berries in acrylic / Prudy Vannier.
—1st ed.
     p.   cm.— (Decorative painting)
   Includes index.
   ISBN 0-89134-935-9 (pbk. : alk. paper)
   1. Fruit in art. 2. Vegetables in art. 3. Acrylic painting—Technique. I. Title. II. Series.
ND1400.V36 1999
751.4′26—dc21   98-38417
                                                           CIP

Editor: Jennifer Long
Production editors: Amanda Magoto and Marilyn Daiker
Production coordinator: Kristen Heller
Cover designer: Brian Roeth
Interior designer: Clare Finney

About the Artist

Prudy Vannier has been teaching art for nearly twenty-five years, specializing in decorative painting since 1986. Not only does she teach nationally and internationally, she also owns and operates Prudy's Studio, Inc. in her hometown of Northville, Michigan, producing decorative painting books by select acrylic artists for painters of all levels. As an educator, Prudy oversees each book, making sure it contains easy instructions and color worksheets for the beginning painter and can be used as a teaching tool for advanced painters. In addition to instructional books, Prudy's Studio carries merchandise just for painters, including apparel, tools and brushes—all designed by Prudy.

Prudy is recognized as a Certified Decorative Artist by the National Society of Decorative Painters, an international organization of over thirty thousand members. She maintains an active seminar schedule and teaches locally near Northville. Watch for Prudy's articles and patterns in tole and decorative painting magazines such as *Tole World*, *PaintWorks*, *Craftworks*, *Decorative Artist's Workbook*, *Crafts*, *Decorative Woodcrafts*, *Painting*, *Let's Paint* and *The Decorative Painter*.

If you have questions or comments, write Prudy at Prudy's Studio, Inc., 279 Maplewood Street, Northville, Michigan 48167-1149, or visit her Web site at www.prudysstudio.com. For a list of patterns, books and merchandise, send a self-addressed stamped envelope to the above address.

Table of Contents

Introduction

Years ago, when I first discovered decorative painting, I wanted to know every technique, every stroke, every "rule" to help me be the best painter I could be. What impatience! I made a notebook containing everything I learned for quick reference, wishing there was already a book like this on the market.

Thus the idea for my first book, *Prudy's Handbook of Classic Fruits*, was born. Then came others: *Guide to Painting Vegetables*, *Beauty of Country Botanicals*, *A Garden Variety* and

more. Every book has patterns, projects and dozens of color step-by-step worksheets for quick reference. Even though several of these books are now out of print, I still get dozens of requests for them.

When Greg Albert, the editorial director of North Light Books, approached me with the idea of publishing a compilation of my earlier books, I thought the idea splendid! (Thank you, Greg!) This is exactly what I wished I had so many years ago when

I was starting decorative painting—sort of an encyclopedia of painting techniques and a reference manual of subjects.

It is my greatest wish that you will be able to use this book as a tool for your own painting growth, no matter what your skill level. Keep it handy as you paint and mark the pages you use most. It is full of hints, suggestions and ideas for your study and perusal. Enjoy!

Supplies for Decorative Painting

PAINTING SURFACES

The designs in this book can be adapted easily to a variety of surfaces, including wood, glass or metal. Use your imagination to visualize a spectacular design on any object.

PAINT

The paints used in this book are Folk-Art acrylic paints; however, I've included a color conversion chart (pages 11–12) for your convenience. As you paint, you will develop favorite colors in many brands. My advice is to stick to the high-quality, reputable brands. If you want to convert into oil paint, I'm afraid you're on your own—my oil painting skills get rustier and rustier the longer I paint in acrylics!

BRUSHES

Good brushes are mandatory for good painting! The most basic brushes needed for decorative painting are: large flats for basecoating, flats or angle brushes for floating shade and highlight colors, mop brushes for softening, a pouncer brush for texture, and liners and rounds for strokework. There are several reputable brush companies such as Loew-Cornell, Scharff, Dove and Royal. My favorite brushes came from many different sources, so I recently had my own brush line produced. They are of the best quality and durability, and best suited for this style of painting.

Prudy's Best Pouncer is similar to a deerfoot brush, but softer and more easily controlled. It is used in this book for drybrushing highlights on fruits and vegetables. It can also be used for "pouncing" foliage and fur.

Prudy's Best Mop is constructed of

Tip
When painting with a liner brush, thin your paint with water slightly, load the brush and paint with your brush as perpendicular to the surface as possible. Gravity helps to pull the thinned paint onto the surface without much reloading for longer, flowing lines.

white goat hair. It is the softest of all mops and best resists water. Use it to soften antiquing and for tint-tiquing (see page 127).

Prudy's Best Liner is constructed with versatility in mind: Its perfect point allows for superfine linework, but there are enough hairs in it to paint a ⅛-inch (.3cm) stripe when you pinch the bottom of the bristles with your fingers. It produces elegant linework and perfect comma strokes. With practice and hand control, you'll find this brush one of your most versatile tools.

Prudy's Best Floater is a ½-inch (1.3cm) synthetic angle brush constructed for holding the exact amount of water and paint needed for floating. I chose the angle cut because of the ease of loading paint into it and for its usefulness in painting small, oddly shaped areas.

Prudy's Best Stroke Brush is a round Kolinsky sable made of natural hairs. The size I chose is the most versatile in painting a wide variety of strokes. Have you had trouble with comma strokes? Usually the problem is solved by finding the brush that is right for you. You'll be amazed at how this brush paints a comma or S-stroke! And it will last for

years if cared for properly.

You will find specialty brushes mentioned in this book. A rake brush is used for multiple lining such as painting wood grain or grass. A filbert is used for some two-color comma strokes. A spotter is best for short, oval-shaped strokes. A disposable foam brush is handy for staining.

OTHER BASIC SUPPLIES

- Sandpaper
- Wood filler
- Tack cloth
- Plastic scouring pad
- Jo Sonja's All Purpose Sealer
- Graphite paper
- Tracing paper
- Masking tape
- Stylus
- Kneaded eraser
- Waxed palette paper
- Water container
- Paper toweling or lint-free rags
- Chalk pencil or soapstone
- Brush cleaner
- Odorless turpentine
- Steel wool
- Toothbrush
- Small sponge
- Waterbase varnish

Tip
Clean natural hair brushes such as a Kolinsky sable in a glass of water, rather than by dragging them across the bottom of a brush basin. Simply tap the brush against the side of the glass and the paint will move to the bottom and wash out of the hairs.

Color Conversion Chart

PLAID FOLKART	DECOART AMERICANA	DELTA CERAMCOAT
758 Alizarin Crimson	Cranberry Wine	Mendocino
715 Amish Blue	French Grey/Blue	Tide Pool Blue
658 Antique Gold Metallic	Venetian Gold	Pale Gold
951 Apple Spice	Crimson Tide + Antique Rose	Tomato Spice + White
646 Aspen Green	Neutral Grey + Hauser Dark Green	Cadmium Grey + Salem Green
920 Autumn Leaves	Burnt Orange	Terra Cotta
938 Barn Wood	Driftwood	Lichen Grey
611 Barnyard Red	Crimson Tide	Burgundy Rose
645 Basil Green	Jade Green	White + Gamal Green
922 Bayberry	Jade Green	Wedgewood Green
719 Blue Ribbon	True Blue	Copen Blue
909 Bluebell	Williamsburg Blue	Bonnie Blue
418 Buckskin Brown	Raw Sienna	Mocha
957 Burgundy	Crimson Tide	Maroon
686 Burnt Carmine	Black Plum	Sonoma + Vintage Wine
943 Burnt Sienna	Terra Cotta	Burnt Sienna
462 Burnt Umber	Burnt Umber	Burnt Umber
939 Butter Pecan	Khaki Tan	Trail
614 Buttercream	Taffy Cream	Custard
905 Buttercup	Golden Straw	Straw
932 Calico Red	Calico Red	Napthol Red Light
758 Cherry Royal	Burgundy Wine	Maroon
958 Christmas Red	Cadmium Red	Fire Red
913 Cinnamon	Shading Flesh	Dark Flesh
601 Clay Bisque	Antique White	Sandstone
923 Clover	Antique Green	Avocado
561 Cobalt Blue	Ultra Blue Deep	Phthalo Blue
926 Cotton Candy	Flesh + Cadmium Red	Indiana Rose
937 Dapple Gray	Neutral Grey	Hippo Gray
426 Dark Gray	Charcoal Grey	Charcoal Grey + Burnt Umber
463 Dioxazine Purple	Dioxazine Purple	Purple
959 English Mustard	Honey Brown	Golden Brown
635 Fuchsia	Royal Fuchsia	Royal Fuchsia
741 Glazed Carrots	Pumpkin	Pumpkin
644 Grass Green	Hauser Light Green	Leaf Green
475 Gray Green	Shale Green	Light Sage
408 Green	Holly Green	Jubilee Green + Phthalo Green
726 Green Meadow	Avocado	Dark Jungle
917 Harvest Gold	Antique Gold	Antique Gold
459 Hauser Green Light	Hauser Light Green	Vibrant Green
460 Hauser Green Medium	Hauser Medium Green	Chrome Green Light
942 Honeycomb	True Ochre	Spice Tan
457 Ice Blue	Dove Grey + Jade Green	Cadet Gray

PLAID FOLKART	DECOART AMERICANA	DELTA CERAMCOAT
908 Indigo	Deep Midnight Blue	Midnight Blue
410 Lavender	Lavender	Lavender
457 Leaf Green	Bright Green	Spring Green
735 Lemon Custard	Lemon Yellow	Bright Yellow
938 Licorice	Ebony Black	Black
425 Light Gray	Dove Grey	Cadet Gray + White
640 Light Periwinkle	Country Blue	Periwinkle
420 Linen	Antique White	Trail + White
412 Magenta	Royal Fuchsia	Royal Fuchsia
945 Maple Syrup	Oxblood	Brown Iron Oxide
944 Nutmeg	Light Cinnamon	Spice Brown
637 Orchid	Orchid	Lilac
575 Payne's Gray	Payne's Gray	Night Fall
413 Pink	Boysenberry + White	White + Berry Red
934 Plum Pudding	Plum	Grape
619 Poetry Green	Green Mist	Green Sea
660 Pure Gold Metallic	Glorious Gold	Metallic Gold
628 Pure Orange	Cadmium Orange	Tangerine
439 Purple Lilac	Summer Lilac	GP Purple + White
638 Purple Passion	Burgundy Wine + True Blue	Napthol Crimson + Liberty Blue
935 Raspberry Wine	Cranberry Wine	Mendocino
452 Raw Sienna	Raw Sienna	Raw Sienna
629 Red Light	Cadmium Red + Cadmium Orange	Crimson
636 Red Violet	Red Violet	Mulberry
952 Ripe Avocado	Antique Green	Avocado
753 Rose Chiffon	Mauve + Dusty Rose	Antique Rose
607 Settler's Blue	French Grey/Blue	Williamsburg Blue
910 Slate Blue	Blueberry + Black	Blue Haze + Midnight
730 Southern Pine	Plantation Pine	Gamal Green
906 Summer Sky	Salem Blue + White	Salem Green + White
918 Sunny Yellow	Lemon Yellow	Bright Yellow
902 Taffy	Buttermilk	Ivory
627 Tangerine	Tangerine	Bittersweet
405 Teal	Teal Green + Veridian	Emerald Green
733 Teal Green	Teal Green	Salem Green
417 Teddy Bear Brown	Light Cinnamon	Autumn Brown
433 Terra Cotta		Terra Cotta
925 Thicket	Avocado + Burnt Umber	Dark Jungle
440 Violet Pansy	Pansy Lavender	Eggplant
649 Warm White	Light Buttermilk	Light Ivory
759 Whipped Berry	Slate Grey	Bridgeport
901 Wicker White	Titanium White	White
963 Wintergreen	Black Forest Green	Phthalo Green
925 Wrought Iron	Black Green	Black Green
918 Yellow Light	Lemon Yellow	Bright Yellow
917 Yellow Ochre	Antique Gold	Antique Gold

Surface Preparation

WOOD

Before painting your wood piece, check it for nail holes or scratches. Fill these with wood filler. My favorite is J.W. etc. Professional Wood Filler. It is water soluble and easy to sand. After filling any flaws in your wood, allow to dry, then sand the entire piece with fine-grit sandpaper. Wipe the piece with a tack cloth to remove dust particles. If your wood is porous and soft, cover with a light coat of wood sealer. If the instructions call for staining, use a rag or foam brush to apply the stain. For a light stain, apply, then wipe off. For a more robust stain, don't wipe off any of the color—you can even apply a second coat if desired. Oil-base stains take a few hours to dry. Acrylic stains are dry in a few minutes.

FABRIC

When painting on fabric, the material must first be washed and dried, using no fabric softeners. Bottled acrylic paint can be used for fabric painting if mixed half and half with textile medium. There are also fabric paints and dyes available in comparable colors. If you love fabric painting, I recommend Debby Forshey's books. They have the most complete fabric instructions of any books I've seen.

PORCELAIN

To prepare porcelain for painting, sand it with extra-fine sandpaper or a plastic scouring pad. Spray with sealer and follow the directions in the pattern to complete.

TIN, OLD METAL, GLASS AND CROCKERY

Old pieces such as fry pans, pots, lamps, spools and the like have a one-of-a-kind charm. To prep the piece, it must be washed and rinsed. If it is rusty, remove as much rust as possible. Rinse again with a vinegar and water solution to remove any oily fingerprints and dirt. Dry thoroughly. I like to place my objects in the oven on warm (under 200°) to ensure all the moisture gets dried out of the rims, cracks and crevices. Paint the piece with Jo Sonja's All Purpose Sealer, following the instructions on the back of the bottle. This is the only product I trust to make the paint adhere to these slick surfaces.

Tip
After applying Jo Sonja's All Purpose Sealer, you can speed up the curing time by placing your object in the oven at 200° or less. The piece should be dry as soon as it has been heated all the way through.

Basecoating and Pattern Transferring

When instructions call for basecoating, always apply two light basecoats rather than one heavy coat. Be sure the first coat is dry before applying the second. If you like the look of wood grain, mix water with the basecoat color to make a thinner paint so the wood will show through. Water makes the grain expand, so be sure to sand the wood piece lightly after it dries before proceeding.

To transfer the pattern to your project, follow these steps:

1. Lay a sheet of tracing paper over the design and trace the pattern. In most cases, it's only necessary to transfer the basic outlines. Small details can be freehanded. Always keep the original design handy for reference as you paint.

2. Position the traced outline on the project to be painted. Secure the tracing with masking tape on one side to hold it in place.

3. Slide the graphite paper under the tracing, shiny side down. Use a stylus to lightly retrace the pattern. Be careful not to press so hard that you indent the lines into the wood. Use dark graphite on light backgrounds and light graphite on dark backgrounds.

Tip
Make it a habit to lighten heavy transfer lines with your kneaded eraser so the lines won't show under the paint.

Painting Techniques

FLOATING

This technique is essential for painting in acrylic. Using the largest flat or angle brush possible, dip your brush into water and blot most of the moisture onto a paper towel. The bristles should be just slightly damp. Dip one corner of the brush into your paint, then stroke it back and forth in one place on your palette paper. This removes excess paint from the edge of your brush and makes the paint blend down toward the clean side of the brush bristles. No paint should touch the clean side of your brush. When you apply the paint to your surface, use the entire width of the brush. Since the paint has been gradually dispersed through the brush, floated strokes will have a "hard" edge (a thicker or more intense application of color) on the loaded edge and a "soft" edge (color that bleeds into the background) on the side painted with the clean edge of the brush.

DOUBLE LOADING

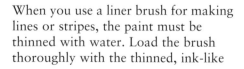

Using a flat angle or filbert brush, dip one side in one color and the other side in a second color. Stroke the brush back and forth in one area of your palette to gradually merge the two colors in the center of your brush. The result will be a two-toned stroke.

LINING

When you use a liner brush for making lines or stripes, the paint must be thinned with water. Load the brush thoroughly with the thinned, ink-like paint. Keep your surface flat and your brush perpendicular to it, holding the brush as straight as possible. This allows gravity to pull the paint onto your surface, creating long, flowing lines and you won't have to reload the brush too often.

Liner brushes come in a vast range of sizes and should be cut to a point—I prefer Prudy's Best Liner or a no. 2 liner. With hand control, several widths of lines can be achieved with a single brush; using a light touch, it's possible to get the ultrafine line of a 10/0 liner. With more pressure and more paint, the heavier line of a no. 6 brush can be achieved.

Problems and Solutions

Problem: My float has hard edges on both sides.
Solution: Either the clean side of your brush has paint in it, or you aren't painting with the entire brush width on the surface of your piece. Be sure you aren't accidentally lifting the clean side of your brush off the surface.

Problem: My paint drags or doesn't cover well.
Solution: You need more water. Don't blot the brush quite so much prior to loading.

Problem: My float is watery and uncontrolled.
Solution: You have too much water in your brush. Take extra care to blot it on a paper towel before sideloading the brush with paint.

Problem: There are "holes" in my floats.
Solution: These are caused by overlapping one float with another before the first layer is dry.

STROKEWORK

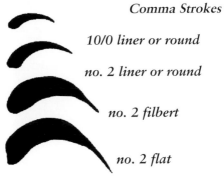

Comma Strokes

10/0 liner or round

no. 2 liner or round

no. 2 filbert

no. 2 flat

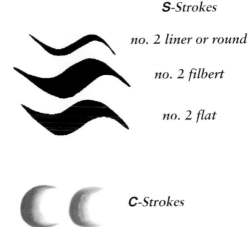

S-Strokes

no. 2 liner or round

no. 2 filbert

no. 2 flat

C-Strokes

One of the most enjoyable techniques in decorative painting is strokework. Once you've mastered it, it's easy and fast to paint a border or small decorative accent on anything. Strokework is done the same way as lining—you can vary the width of lines by adjusting the amount of pressure you use. Different brushes will also give you slightly different effects. Find the brush that's right for you—one that allows you to make the best strokes possible for the type of stroke you want to paint—whether it's a flat, filbert, round or liner brush. My favorite brush for strokework is a round Kolinsky sable, such as Prudy's Best Stroke Brush. Load your brush with creamy, slightly thinned paint and experiment with getting a variety of lines or strokes by adjusting the pressure you use. Notice that you will have "meaty" strokes when you press hard, and light, narrow lines when your touch is light. Comma strokes and S-strokes are made by simply loading your brush and using the correct amount of pressure on the brush to achieve the shape you want. C-strokes are done by sideloading a flat brush and painting a C shape.

BRUSH TIP DOTS

Dip the handle end of the brush into a fresh puddle of paint and tap it on your surface to make a dot. Smaller handles make smaller dots (makes sense, doesn't it?). A stylus makes an itty-bitty dot. For dots that change in size, make a series of dots before reloading your handle—the dots will get progressively smaller as you run out of paint.

TINTING

Tinting gives just a suggestion of color. Use it as a tool for creating color harmony throughout your painting; look carefully at a floral painting and you will see subtle greens in the roses petals and reds in the leaves. Float tint colors with very thin paint. Adding suggestions of color to your background is called tint-tiquing. See page 127.

HIGHLIGHTING

To create the illusion of a highlight, apply a color lighter than the basecoat on the side of the object closest to the light source. The intense highlight is the spot on the object where the light hits. It is painted with a "warm white" such as Taffy, Clay Bisque or Warm White. The intense highlight can be floated, but often—especially on rounded objects such as fruit—it is drybrushed by pouncing with a deerfoot stippler or Prudy's Best Pouncer.

SHADING

To help create dimension, the side of the object farthest from the light source is shaded by painting it with a color darker than the basecoat. This color is usually floated with a flat or angle brush.

REFLECTED LIGHT

Picture an apple hanging on a tree. The sunlight hits the front of the apple, creating a warm highlight. The sunlight also shines on the foliage and other objects surrounding the apple, including the areas behind your apple. The light that bounces off those leaves and other objects and back onto the backside of your apple is called reflected light. Paint reflected light on the edge of an object (such as your apple), opposite the intense highlight. Use a "cool white" since the source of this light is not the warm sunshine. I usually paint the reflected light with Whipped Berry, Settler's Blue or a similar light blue-gray.

Painting Fruit & Berries

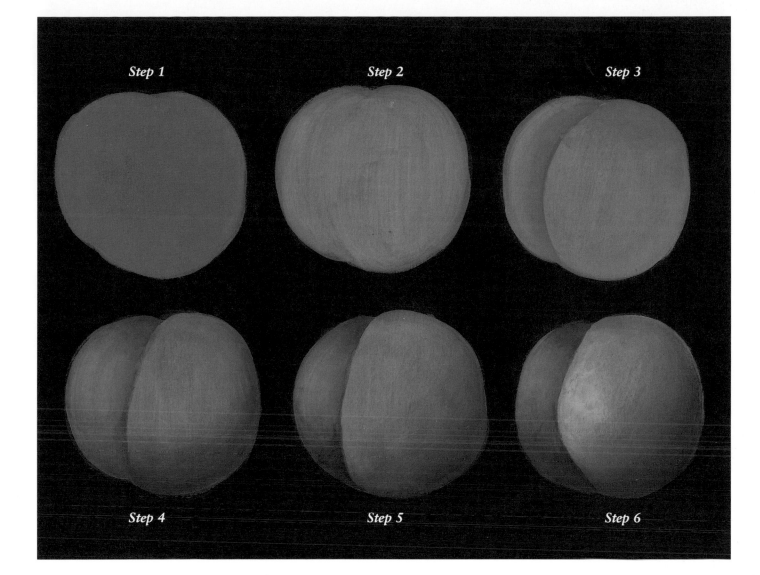

Step 1 Step 2 Step 3

Step 4 Step 5 Step 6

Painting Peaches

FolkArt Colors
Alizarin Crimson
Burnt Carmine
Buttercup
Clay Bisque
English Mustard
Glazed Carrots
Settler's Blue

1. Basecoat the peaches with Glazed Carrots. Let dry.

2. Thin Buttercup with water and wash over the peach.

3. Establish your light source. On the worksheet above, the light source is on the left, so the shading is on the right. Float English Mustard to establish the shading and the crevice in the peach.

4. Deepen the shading and "blush" the peach by floating Alizarin Crimson.

5. Float Burnt Carmine to darken the shading at the top and bottom of the crevice and on the darkest side of the peach (the left side in this example.)

6. Highlight the peach by drybrush-

Tip
When painting a project that includes fruit, use the following instructions and worksheets for the type of fruit desired, unless otherwise directed in the individual project instructions.

ing or lightly pouncing Clay Bisque in the highlight area. This gives the peach a soft texture. Add the reflected light with a float of Settler's Blue against the dark edge.

Painting Apples

FolkArt Colors
Burnt Carmine
Burnt Umber
Buttercup
Calico Red
Clay Bisque
Raspberry Wine
Settler's Blue

APPLE # 1

1. Basecoat the apple with Buttercup. On a dark surface, this might take several coats. Using an angle brush, float Calico Red around the edge.

2. With the same brush, float a U across the top to make the stem end of the apple. (Use this same kind of float to make the blossom end as shown on Apple #2.)

3. Establish your light source. Decide where your highlight area will be on each apple. Circle this area with a chalk pencil if necessary. Sideload an angle brush with Calico Red and float around the apple to fill it in, except on the highlight area. Always keep the clean side of the brush toward the highlight area so it remains yellow. It will take several coats of Calico Red to redden the apple enough before you go on to the shading. Be patient and allow the paint to dry between floats.

4. Shade the apple with floats of Raspberry Wine.

5. Deepen the shading on the darkest side of the apple with Burnt Carmine.

6. Heighten the highlight area with Clay Bisque. Add reflected light with a float of Settler's Blue on the dark side.

7. Paint the stem with Burnt Umber and add a Clay Bisque highlight.

APPLE #2

1. These apples are turned slightly to show the blossom ends. Basecoat with Buttercup as above and float Calico Red around the apples. Paint the blossom area on the first apple on the left by floating Calico Red against the top of the blossom area and across the bottom. Paint the blossom end on the second apple (on the right) with the same U stroke used in Apple #1.

2. Fill in both apples with Calico Red, keeping the highlight areas clean. Be careful to keep the highlight round on the apple on the right. It's easy to mistakenly float against the apple on top of it and end up with a triangular-shaped highlight.

3. Using Raspberry Wine, shade the dark sides of each apple, on the second apple where it is overlapped, and on the inside of the blossom end on the first apple.

4. Deepen the shading on the second apple with Burnt Carmine.

5. Highlight both apples with Clay Bisque. This should be brighter on the apple on the left. Add the reflected light with a float of Settler's Blue on the dark sides of both apples.

6. Paint the blossom ends with dots or tiny strokes of Burnt Umber. Highlight with dots of Buttercup.

Painting Blossoms & Berries

FolkArt Colors
Alizarin Crimson
Burnt Carmine
Calico Red
English Mustard
Glazed Carrots
Hauser Green Light
Hauser Green Medium
Nutmeg
Southern Pine
Taffy
Warm White
Wicker White
Yellow Light

1. Basecoat the petals with Taffy, the center with English Mustard, the leaves and stems with Hauser Green Medium and the berries with Calico Red.

2. Shade the petals and berries by floating Alizarin Crimson, and the leaves with Southern Pine. Shade around the center and create its form with Nutmeg.

3. Highlight the petals with Wicker White, the berries with Glazed Carrots, the leaves with Hauser Green Light and the center with Yellow Light.

4. Deep shade the petals with Burnt Carmine. Add shine marks to the berries and intensify the highlights in the centers with Warm White.

5. Tint the edges of the petals with Yellow Light and Glazed Carrots. Paint the lines radiating from the center with thinned Burnt Carmine, then dot with Yellow Light, Glazed Carrots and Alizarin Crimson. Dot the berries with Burnt Carmine.

Step 1

Step 2

Step 3

APPLE #1

Step 4

Step 5

Steps 6 & 7

Step 1

Step 2

APPLE #2

Steps 3 & 4

Steps 5 & 6

PAINTING PLUMS

FolkArt Colors
- Alizarin Crimson
- Amish Blue
- Clay Bisque
- Indigo
- Settler's Blue
- Slate Blue

1. Basecoat the plums with Amish Blue. Shade by floating around the plum with Slate Blue. Establish the crevice in the plum by floating against both sides: float down one side, turn your brush over and float up the other side.

2. Establish the position of the highlight by the direction of the light source. The light on the plums on the worksheet is coming from the left. Using a ½-inch (1.3cm) flat or angle brush, fill in the plum with Slate Blue, except on the highlight area. Layer the floats until the plum is mostly Slate Blue, allowing it to dry between floats.

3. Shade the plum with Indigo, using the same method as in step 2.

4. Thin Alizarin Crimson with water and wash over the plum, creating a tint.

5. Highlight the plum with Clay Bisque.

6. Add reflected light on the dark edge of the plum with a float of Settler's Blue.

PAINTING GRAPES

FolkArt Colors
- Alizarin Crimson
- Burnt Carmine
- Burnt Umber
- Butter Pecan
- Buttercup
- Clay Bisque
- Clover
- Honeycomb
- Nutmeg
- Ripe Avocado
- Settler's Blue
- Terra Cotta

1. The darkest grapes are those peeking out from under the bunch here and there. They are lettered **A** on the worksheet. Basecoat these with Butter Pecan.

The middle value grapes are labeled **B**. Basecoat them with Honeycomb. The lightest grapes in the bunch, those on top or closest to the light source, are labeled **C**. Basecoat these with Buttercup. The tiny, unripe grapes at the end of the bunch are labeled **D**. Basecoat them with Honeycomb. The following instructions are given for the lettered grapes on the worksheet. When painting your own grapes, the arrangement of the colors is totally dependent on your own preference.

2. *Grape A*—Shade by floating Terra Cotta, leaving the area closest to the light source the basecoat color.
Grape B—Shade by floating Burnt Carmine.
Grape C—Shade with Terra Cotta.
Grape D—Float Terra Cotta on the right sides of the grapes.

3. *Grape A*—Deep shade with Burnt Carmine.
Grape B—Deep shade where they are overlapped with another float of Burnt Carmine.
Grape C—Float over the Terra Cotta shading with a wash of Alizarin Crimson.
Grape D—Float down the left side of the grapes with Burnt Carmine.

4. Paint in the stems with Nutmeg, using a liner brush.

5. *Grape A*—Deepen the shading where these grapes are overlapped with another float of Burnt Carmine.
Grape B—Highlight with Clay Bisque.
Grape C—Deep shade with Burnt Carmine.
Grape D—Float across the bottom with Ripe Avocado.

6. Highlight all the stems here and there with Honeycomb.

7. *Grape A*—No highlights on these grapes.
Grape B—Float reflected light on the dark edge of each grape with Settler's Blue.
Grape C and *D*—Highlight with Clay Bisque. Float reflected light with Settler's Blue.

8. Shade the stems here and there with Burnt Umber using a liner brush.

9. Basecoat the grape leaves with Clover and use the general leaf instructions on pages 30-31 to shade and highlight.

PAINTING CHERRIES

FolkArt Colors
- Burnt Carmine
- Calico Red
- Clay Bisque
- Grass Green
- Green Meadow
- Honeycomb
- Nutmeg
- Raspberry Wine
- Settler's Blue
- Yellow Ochre

1. Basecoat the cherries with a mix of Yellow Ochre + Clay Bisque.

2. Float Calico Red around the outside edges all the way around. Let dry and then float Calico Red in a U shape at the top to form the stem end.

3. Redden the cherries by floating and refloating Calico Red, leaving the highlight area clean.

4. Paint the stems with Grass Green, using a liner brush.

5. Shade the cherries with floats of Raspberry Wine. Shade the stems with Green Meadow where they go into the cherries.

6. Deep shade with Burnt Carmine on the back cherry where it is overlapped. Highlight with Clay Bisque.

7. Float reflected light on the dark side of both cherries with Settler's Blue.

8. Connect the stems at the end with a larger, darker stem using Nutmeg and highlight it slightly with Honeycomb.

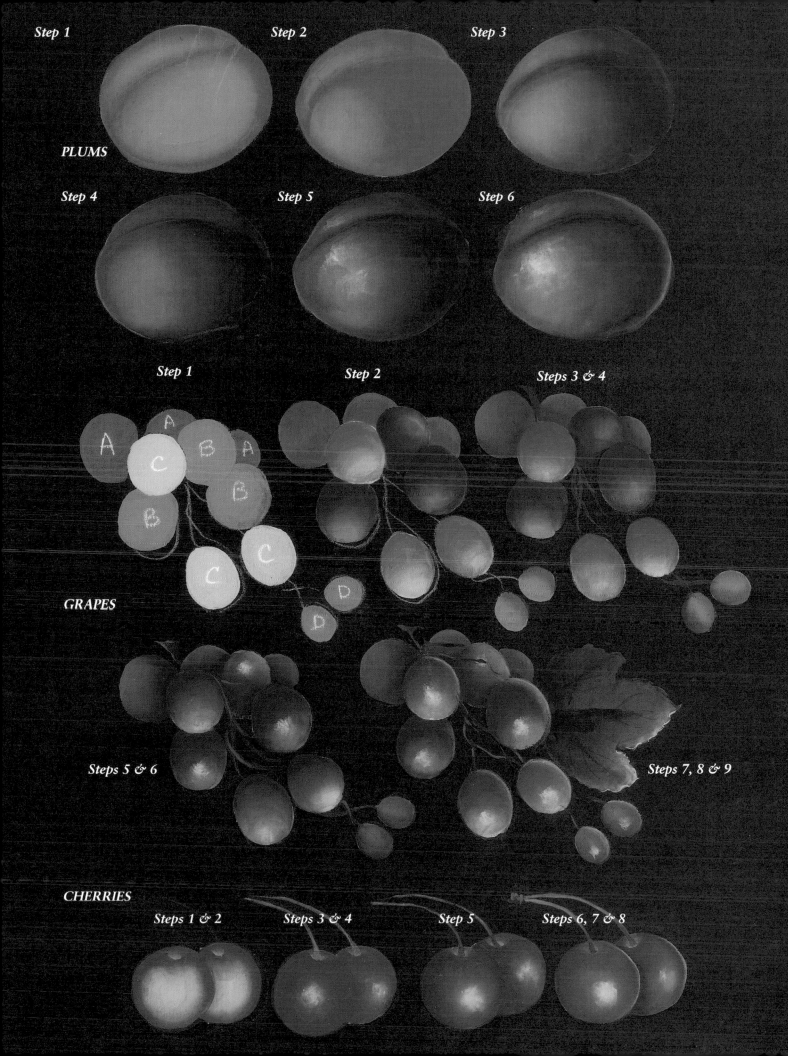

PLUMS

Step 1   Step 2   Step 3

Step 4   Step 5   Step 6

GRAPES

Step 1   Step 2   Steps 3 & 4

A A B B A
C B
C C
D D

Steps 5 & 6   Steps 7, 8 & 9

CHERRIES

Steps 1 & 2   Steps 3 & 4   Step 5   Steps 6, 7 & 8

Painting Pears

1. Basecoat the pears with Yellow Ochre, then float around the entire edge of the pear with Burnt Sienna using a ¼-inch (.6cm) angle brush.

2. Using the same brush, float a U shape with Burnt Sienna to make the stem end.

3. Decide which side of the pear will be the light side containing the highlight area. (The pear on the worksheet has its light source coming from the left.) Shade the pear on the opposite side with layers of Burnt Sienna floats. Use a ½-inch (1.3cm) angle brush to apply the shading; it gets the job done faster and easier.

4. After the Burnt Sienna is thoroughly dry, deepen the shading on the dark side of the pear with a float of Maple Syrup.

5. Again deepen the shading slightly with a float of Burnt Umber.

6. Highlight the pear on the light side with Clay Bisque. Add reflected light by floating Settler's Blue along the dark side.

7. Paint the stems on the pears with Burnt Umber. These should be thicker than the delicate apple stems. Highlight the stems with a touch of Yellow Ochre.

8. Pears can be "blushed" for interest or to make them fit better in a specific color scheme. Any color of red or burgundy will do. The double pears on the worksheet are floated with Alizarin Crimson. I usually apply this "blush" on the lower ends and on the shaded side. These pears are turned up so the blossom ends show. This angle often lends more interest to a grouping of fruit. To emphasize the angle, float the shade color on the upper inside of the blossom end area.

9. When pears overlap, the lower one has to be darker since the upper one will be casting a shadow onto it. Simply deepen the shading on the lower pear by floating Burnt Umber where the top pear overlaps. The reflected light on both pears is the same. The highlight on the upper pear should be brighter than on the lower pear.

10. Paint the blossom end with dots of Burnt Umber mixed with Licorice. Highlight with a few dots of Yellow Ochre.

Painting Blueberries

1. Basecoat the blueberries solidly with Amish Blue.

2. Establish your light source. Which side of your berries will be shaded? My light source on the worksheet is on the left side. Shade each berry where appropriate with floats of Slate Blue. Remember to shade the back berries more than the ones in the front, particularly where they are overlapped.

3. Deepen the shading with floats of Indigo.

4. Some or all of your berries can be tinted. Use Alizarin Crimson mixed with water to make a wash and apply the tints as shown on the worksheet.

5. Highlight the blueberries with Clay Bisque.

6. To make the blossom ends, double load a no. 2 flat brush with Clay Bisque on one side and Indigo on the other. Palette blend slightly. Make a blossom end with one small stroke. The Indigo side of the brush goes on the light side of the berry, while the Clay Bisque side of the brush goes toward the dark side. Remember to vary the positions of the blossom ends on the berries for more interest.

7. Highlight the edges of the blossom ends here and there with Clay Bisque using a liner brush. Finally, float Settler's Blue on the shaded side of each berry for reflected light.

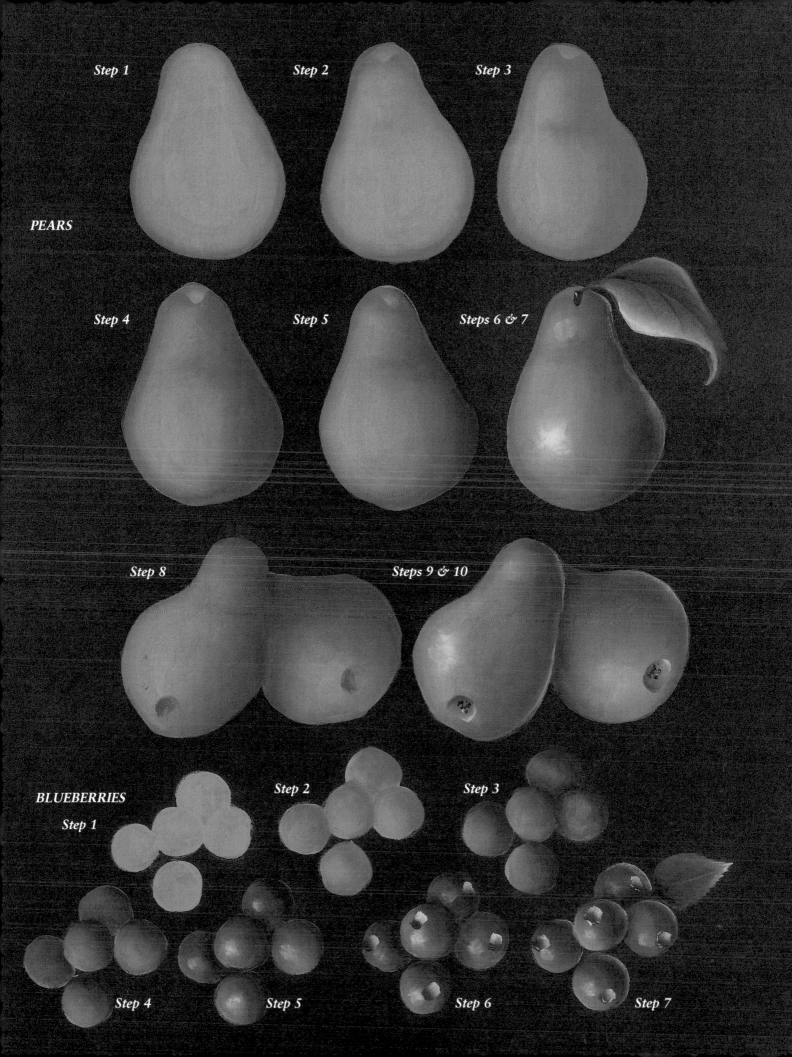

PEARS

Step 1 Step 2 Step 3

Step 4 Step 5 Steps 6 & 7

Step 8 Steps 9 & 10

BLUEBERRIES

Step 1 Step 2 Step 3

Step 4 Step 5 Step 6 Step 7

Painting Berries

GOOSEBERRIES

FolkArt Colors
Alizarin Crimson
Burnt Umber
Butter Pecan
Clay Bisque
Clover
Settler's Blue
Wrought Iron

1. Basecoat the gooseberries with Butter Pecan.

2. Establish your light source. Now shade each berry opposite the light source with floats of Clover. The berries that overlap each other should have more Clover and then be deep shaded with floats of Wrought Iron.

3. Paint the stripes on each berry with Butter Pecan thinned with water using a liner brush. Plan the stripes so they intersect at the blossom end. It is helpful to sketch in the stripes with a chalk pencil before painting.

4. Tint each berry across the light areas with a wash of Alizarin Crimson mixed with water.

5. Stroke in the branch with Burnt Umber.

6. Highlight the gooseberries with Clay Bisque. Add the reflected light with a float of Settler's Blue on the dark edge of each berry. Paint the blossom ends with tiny strokes of Burnt Umber.

7. Highlight the branch and make "prickers" with Butter Pecan.

BLACKBERRIES

FolkArt Colors
Alizarin Crimson
Clay Bisque
Grass Green
Green Meadow
Settler's Blue
Violet Pansy
Yellow Ochre

1. Basecoat the blackberries with Yellow Ochre, keeping the edges soft (fuzzy).

2. Give the berries a wash of thinned Alizarin Crimson.

3. Double load a tiny flat brush (no. 1 or no. 2) with Settler's Blue and Violet Pansy. With the gray edge of the brush out, make individual circles to form the segments of the berry. Start at the edges and do the center last. I rarely use painting mediums but, if you're having trouble getting smooth circles, you might try coating the berry with a thin layer of FolkArt Extender.

4. Establish your light source and then wash over the shaded side of the berry with thinned Indigo.

5. Highlight the segments on the light side of the berries with floats of Clay Bisque.

6. Highlight the light segments again with dots of Clay Bisque. Add reflected light on the dark segments by lining the shaded side of each with Settler's Blue.

7. Paint the calyx with lines of Green Meadow, then Grass Green. Let dry and then add tiny lines of Yellow Ochre over the top of the calyx.

RASPBERRIES

FolkArt Colors
Alizarin Crimson
Buttercup
Clay Bisque
Grass Green
Green Meadow
Raspberry Wine
Settler's Blue
Terra Cotta

1. Basecoat the raspberries with Buttercup, keeping the edges soft.

2. Give the raspberries a thinned wash of Alizarin Crimson.

3. Double load a tiny flat brush (no. 1 or no. 2) with Alizarin Crimson on one side and Terra Cotta on the other. With the Terra Cotta on the outside, make individual circles to form the segments of the berry, starting on the edges and working toward the middle. You might find it helpful to coat the berry with FolkArt Extender before making the circles.

4. Establish your light source, then wash over the shaded side of the berries with thinned Raspberry Wine.

5. Highlight the segments on the light side of the berry with Buttercup.

6. Highlight the light segments again with dots of Clay Bisque. Add reflected light on the dark segments by lining the shaded side of each with Settler's Blue.

7. Paint the calyx with lines of Green Meadow, then Grass Green. Let dry and then add tiny lines of thinned Buttercup over the top of the calyx.

STRAWBERRIES

FolkArt Colors
Bayberry
Burnt Carmine
Calico Red
Clay Bisque
Grass Green
Green Meadow
Licorice
Raspberry Wine
Yellow Ochre

1. Basecoat the strawberries with a mix of Yellow Ochre + Clay Bisque. Redden the berries by floating with Calico Red, leaving the basecoat showing in the highlight and unripe areas.

2. Shade the strawberry with Raspberry Wine.

3. Deep shade with Burnt Carmine on the back berry where it is overlapped. Float Grass Green on the tip of the unripe berry.

4. Load the corner of a flat brush with Raspberry Wine and smudge where each seed will go.

5. Using a liner brush and thinned Bayberry, place the seeds in the smudged spots.

6. Highlight the berries with Clay Bisque. The front berry should have more of a highlight. Add reflected light by floating Settler's Blue on the shaded side of each berry.

7. Paint the calyx leaves with Grass Green and Green Meadow double loaded on a small flat brush. Stroke the calyx leaves in one at a time.

GOOSEBERRIES

Step 1   Step 2   Step 3

Steps 4 & 5   Steps 6 & 7

RASPBERRIES & BLACKBERRIES

Step 1   Step 2   Step 3

Step 4   Step 5   Steps 6 & 7

STRAWBERRIES

Step 1   Step 2

Steps 3 & 4   Step 5   Steps 6 & 7

RED CURRANTS

FolkArt Colors
Alizarin Crimson
Buttercup
Calico Red
Cinnamon
Clover
Hauser Green Light
Honeycomb
Leaf Green
Pure Orange
Raspberry Wine
Settler's Blue
Southern Pine
Warm White
Wrought Iron

1. Basecoat the dominant berries with Buttercup, the berries in the background with Cinnamon, and the unripe berries with Honeycomb. The fronts of the leaves and stems are Leaf Green. The backs of the leaves are Hauser Green Light.

2. Shade the yellow berries by floating Pure Orange across the backs. This should cover at least two-thirds of the berry. Float Clover across the bottoms of the unripe berries. Shade the leaves and stems by floating Southern Pine under the flips and around the veins.

3. Float Calico Red on the yellow berries. Float Alizarin Crimson across the top of each unripe berry. Deepen the leaf shading with Wrought Iron.

4. Shade the main berries and background berries with Raspberry Wine. Highlight the edges of the leaves with transparent floats of Warm White.

5. Line the berries with thinned Warm White.

6. Add highlights of Warm White, reflected light with Settler's Blue and blossom ends with Wrought Iron.

BLACK CURRANTS

FolkArt Colors
Alizarin Crimson
Burnt Carmine
Clover
Hauser Green Light
Honeycomb
Leaf Green
Purple Lilac
Settler's Blue
Southern Pine
Violet Pansy
Warm White
Wrought Iron

1. Basecoat the berries with Violet Pansy.

2. Shade across the tops with Burnt Carmine. Highlight across the bottoms with Purple Lilac.

3. Line with thinned Purple Lilac.

4. Add reflected light with Settler's Blue and highlight with Warm White. Paint the blossom ends with Wrought Iron.

Tip
The leaves, stems and unripe berries for the black currants are done in exactly the same way as for the red currants.

RASPBERRIES ON RASPBERRY MUFFIN TABLE (pages 64–66)

FolkArt Colors
Alizarin Crimson
Burnt Umber
Clover
Hauser Green Light
Raspberry Wine
Ripe Avocado
Settler's Blue
Southern Pine
Warm White
Wrought Iron
Yellow Ochre

1. Basecoat the berry shapes with Yellow Ochre. Basecoat the leaves, stems and calyxes with Clover.

2. Thin Alizarin Crimson with water and wash over the berry shapes. Paint the back sides of the leaves that show as flips with Hauser Green Light.

3. Use Alizarin Crimson to make each dot on the berries. Float Hauser Green Light on the fronts of the leaves to brighten. Line the stems and calyxes with this on the light side.

4. Thin Raspberry Wine with water. Sideload and wash over the dark sides of the berries. Float the center vein areas of the leaves with thinned Southern Pine. Paint the large thorns with Yellow Ochre. The smaller ones are Ripe Avocado.

5. Mix Raspberry Wine plus a touch of Wrought Iron. Shade each individual dot by floating this on the dark side. Establish veins in the leaves by floating around them with thinned Southern Pine.

6. Float thinned Warm White on the light side of each dot. Line the dark sides with Settler's Blue to make reflected light. Line the berry "bud" with thinned Burnt Umber. The dark sides of the gold thorns are lined with Burnt Umber. Deepen the shading on the leaves with Wrought Iron.

7. Make shine lights on berries by dotting with Warm White. Dot the berry "bud" with Burnt Umber. Use a rake brush to stripe the leaves with Hauser Green Light. Highlight some leaf edges with Warm White. Tint with Alizarin Crimson.

RED CURRANTS

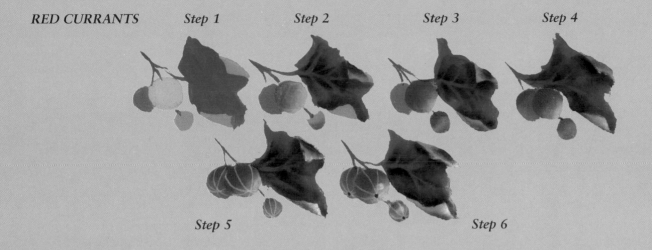

Step 1   Step 2   Step 3   Step 4

Step 5   Step 6

BLACK CURRANTS

Step 1   Step 2   Step 3   Step 4

RASPBERRIES (pages 64–66)

Step 1   Step 2   Step 3

Step 4   Step 5   Step 6   Step 7

WILD STRAWBERRIES

FolkArt Colors
Bayberry
Calico Red
Glazed Carrots
Hauser Green Light
Hauser Green Medium
Leaf Green
Licorice
Nutmeg
Southern Pine
Warm White
Yellow Light

1. Basecoat the unripe berries with Hauser Green Light and the ripe berry with Yellow Light. The leaves and stems are Bayberry.

2. Float the following colors across the base of the berries according to ripeness: Leaf Green, Glazed Carrots and Calico Red. Float Hauser Green Medium across the base of each leaf.

3. Highlight the berries with Warm White. Float this on the tips of the leaves and calyxes also.

4. Use a liner brush with Licorice to add seeds.

5. Add root "leaves" with Bayberry and Leaf Green and veins with thinned Southern Pine.

6. Paint the roots with Nutmeg.

OLIVE BERRIES

FolkArt Colors
Clover
Dioxazine Purple
Hauser Green Light
Nutmeg
Settler's Blue
Violet Pansy
Warm White
Wrought Iron

1. Basecoat the berries with Violet Pansy and the leaves and stem with Clover.

2. Float Dioxazine Purple at the base of each berry. Shade the leaves by floating Wrought Iron under the slips and where one leaf is on top of another.

3. Use a liner brush with thinned Warm White to add dots to the berries. Highlight the edges of the leaves and paint the veins with Hauser Green Light.

4. Make shine marks on the berries with Warm White and intensify the highlights on the leaves with the same. Add reflected light with Settler's Blue. Add Nutmeg strokes at the bases of the berries.

COFFEE BERRIES

FolkArt Colors
Burnt Carmine
Calico Red
Clover
Glazed Carrots
Hauser Green Light
Settler's Blue
Warm White
Wrought Iron

1. Basecoat the berries with Calico Red.

2. Shade at the bases of each berry by floating Burnt Carmine. Lighten the opposite ends by floating Glazed Carrots.

3. Highlight with Warm White. Add reflected light with Settler's Blue.

4. The ends are thinned Burnt Carmine.

WHORTLE BERRIES & BLUEBERRIES

FolkArt Colors
Alizarin Crimson
Hauser Green Light
Indigo
Leaf Green
Settler's Blue
Warm White
Whipped Berry
Wrought Iron

1. Basecoat the berries with Settler's Blue and the stems and leaves with Leaf Green.

2. Shade the berries on the dark sides with floats of Indigo. Shade the base of each leaf by lightly floating Wrought Iron.

3. Highlight the light sides of the berries with Whipped Berry. Highlight the tips of the leaves and some parts of the stems with Hauser Green Light.

4. Double load a no. 2 flat brush with Indigo on one side and Settler's Blue on the other. Palette-blend slightly, then paint the blossom end of each berry. Do this by laying the dark side of the brush on the light side of the berry.

5. Tint a few of the berries by washing over with thinned Alizarin Crimson. Add some tints to the leaves, too.

6. Highlight the berries and edges of the blossom ends with Warm White. Add reflected light to the dark sides of the berries with Settler's Blue.

ROSE HIPS

FolkArt Colors
Burnt Carmine
Burnt Umber
Calico Red
Dapple Gray
Glazed Carrots
Licorice
Settler's Blue
Terra Cotta
Warm White

1. Basecoat the berries with Calico Red and the stems with Terra Cotta.

2. Shade the berries by floating Burnt Carmine across the backs. Shade the stems by lining with Burnt Umber.

3. Highlight the berries with Glazed Carrots. Paint the calyx ends with Licorice.

4. Intensify highlights with Warm White. Add Dapple Gray and Licorice lines and dots at the ends. Reflected light is Settler's Blue.

Tip
Coffee leaves and stems are painted exactly like the olive leaves.

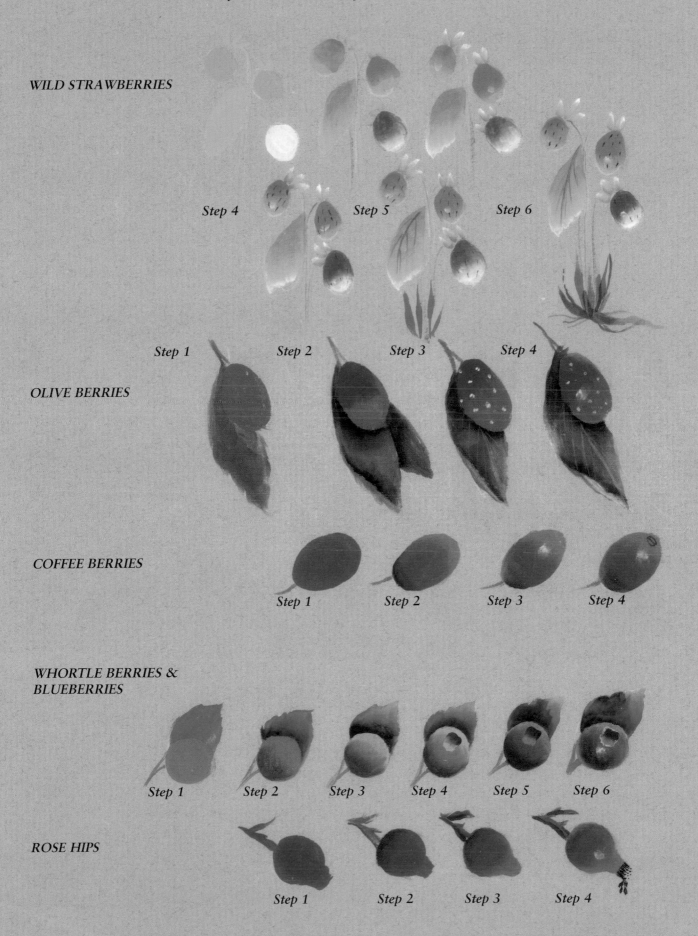

WILD STRAWBERRIES

Step 1 Step 2 Step 3

Step 4 Step 5 Step 6

OLIVE BERRIES

Step 1 Step 2 Step 3 Step 4

COFFEE BERRIES

Step 1 Step 2 Step 3 Step 4

WHORTLE BERRIES & BLUEBERRIES

Step 1 Step 2 Step 3 Step 4 Step 5 Step 6

ROSE HIPS

Step 1 Step 2 Step 3 Step 4

Painting Leaves

THE BASIC LEAVES

FolkArt Colors
Medium green of your choice (Basecoat the leaves with any medium green. I used Green Meadow in the worksheet examples. For a more neutral leaf, such as the grape and gooseberry leaves, use Clover.)
Clay Bisque
Grass Green
Wrought Iron

1. Basecoat with the medium green of your choice.
2. Highlight by floating Grass Green, starting at the tip and working a fourth to halfway up the leaf. Also highlight along the center vein. Grass Green is bright, but quiets down when you get the next highlight on it. If you prefer more subdued leaves, use Bayberry for your highlights.
3. Shade with Wrought Iron starting at the back of the leaf and working toward the front. On a dark surface this is a great shade color for leaves. If you are working on a light background use Thicket for this step.
4. Brighten the highlight with a float of Clay Bisque. On a light background, lighten the highlight with Grass Green + Wicker White, or Bayberry + Wicker White.
5. Line the edge in the highlight area with the highlight color to sharpen it. Add veins with the deep shade color if desired. (Wrought Iron in the worksheet example). Using color from the fruits around it, tint the leaf here and there with washes.

TURNED LEAVES

1. Begin painting the leaf as directed in steps 1 through 3 for the basic leaf.
2. First decide where your flips will be. Remember that your most detailed leaves should not stray far from the center of interest in your painting. Use a chalk pencil to draw the flips. Float your deepest shade color against the flip to form it. (Wrought Iron was used in the worksheet example).
3. Highlight the edge of the flip with your highlight color. Add more detail if you like by using the highlight color to form ridges on the edge of the leaf.
4. Add veins and tint as directed in step 5 for the basic leaf.

BUG HOLES IN LEAVES

Bug holes add even more detail and interest in a painting and are great fun! Remember to add them only to the leaves around your center of interest. They can very easily be added as an afterthought.
1. Paint the basic leaf as described above.
2. Paint a hole in the edge of your leaf using the background color. Highlight the edge of the hole here and there with your highlight color. I used Clay Bisque on the worksheet example. Tint and vein as described above.

TENDRILS

Tendrils give a feeling of lightness and delicacy to a painting. They can be straight, gently curved or kinky, and they can be separate or intertwined. By placing them strategically to point in a certain direction, they can also be used as a tool to direct the viewer's eye. Tendrils are often used in this way at the edge of a design to lead the eye back into the design. Alternately, sometimes the wood surface that holds the design is so interesting, a tendril will guide the viewer's eye to examine the surface as well as the design on it.
1. Use a chalk pencil to draw the tendrils first if you like, but use this line only as a guide to show the general direction that the tendril will flow. If you try too hard to follow your pattern line, the tendril will look forced and not as graceful.
2. To paint a tendril, use a green or green mix that is already on your palette and add water to thin the paint to an inky consistency. Saturate a small liner brush (I prefer a 10/0) and, holding your brush perpendicular to the painting, line the tendril. Holding your brush straight allows gravity to draw the paint off the brush; you will also get a finer line if you paint on the very tip. Adding more pressure to your brush will create a thicker line.

PAINTING DEWDROPS

Dewdrops add interest to the focal point of a painting. With a little practice they are easy and fun to do. When planning them in your painting, there are a few things to remember:
• You can use more than one dewdrop, but be sure they are within your center of interest. A dewdrop off to the side is distracting, but one or more placed correctly add detail and charm to the focal point area.
• Place dewdrops in the middle value area of the fruit or leaf, not in the deep shade area or the highlight area.

1. Draw a basic "fish hook" shape on the fruit or leaf to use as a guide. I prefer a chalk pencil that is easily erased. The angle of the dewdrop might vary depending on the shape and curvature of the fruit. Using the highlight color (Clay Bisque on the worksheet example), float the shape. This is the bright side of the dewdrop so it should be facing the light source.
2. Using the shade color of the fruit or leaf, float under the dewdrop and up the opposite side of the first float. On a pear this would be Maple Syrup or Burnt Umber; on an apple it would be Raspberry Wine or Raspberry Wine + Licorice; on a blueberry or plum it would be Indigo. Get the idea?
3. With a liner brush, add reflected light on the dewdrop opposite the first float.

BASIC LEAVES

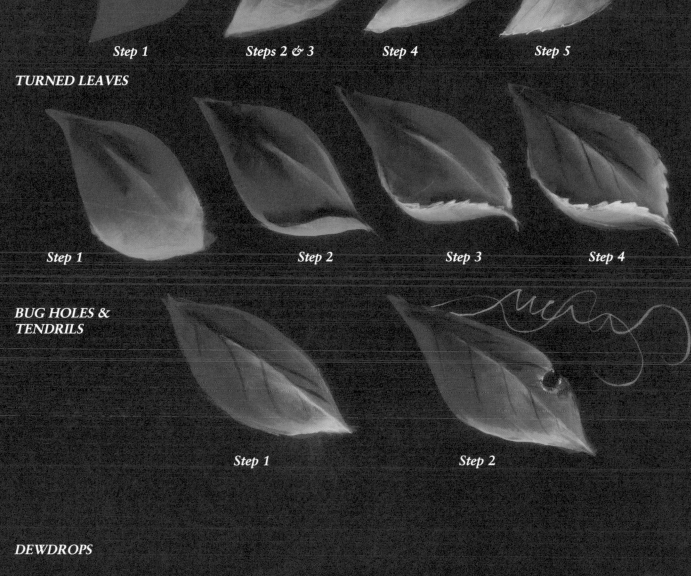

Step 1   Steps 2 & 3   Step 4   Step 5

TURNED LEAVES

Step 1   Step 2   Step 3   Step 4

BUG HOLES & TENDRILS

Step 1   Step 2

DEWDROPS

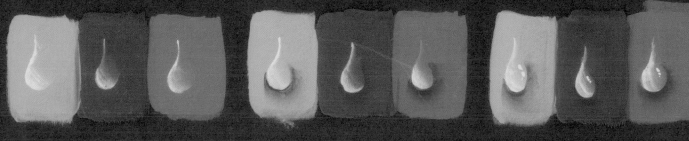

Step 1   Step 2   Step 3

Apple Cider Time

Surface Source

This 9-inch-high (22.9cm) crockery pitcher was manufactured by Robinson Ramsbottom Pottery, P.O. Box 7, Roseville, OH 43777. Phone (614) 697-7355. Check your local hardware or variety stores for a similar pitcher.

FolkArt Colors

Apples
  Burnt Umber
  Buttercup
  Calico Red
  Clay Bisque
  Raspberry Wine
  Settler's Blue

Leaves
  Buttercup
  Clay Bisque
  Grass Green
  Green Meadow or medium
    green of your choice
  Wrought Iron

Other Supplies
  Jo Sonja's All Purpose Sealer

1. Prepare the pitcher according to the instructions for porcelain found on page 13.

2. Transfer the apple pattern.

3. Paint the apples as instructed on pages 18-19. Paint the leaves as instructed on pages 30-31, with one exception: highlight the leaves with Buttercup so that they show up better on the creamy background of the crock.

Prudy's Peachy Tray

Surface Source
This 19″ × 9½″ (49.5cm × 24.1cm) wooden tray is available from Allen's Wood Crafts, 3020 Dogwood Lane, Rt. 3, Sapulpa, OK 74066. Phone (918) 224-8796.

FolkArt Colors

Peaches
Alizarin Crimson
Buttercup
Clay Bisque
English Mustard
Glazed Carrots
Licorice
Settler's Blue

Leaves and Branch
Burnt Umber
Clay Bisque
Grass Green
Green Meadow or medium green of your choice
Nutmeg
Wrought Iron
Yellow Ochre

Other Supplies
FolkArt Waterbase Antiquing Wood 'N' Bucket Brown
Minwax Cherry Wood Finish
Minwax Early American Wood Finish

1. Sand the wooden tray and wipe with a tack cloth.

2. Stain the back and edges of the tray as instructed on page 13, using Wood 'N' Bucket Brown antiquing and Minwax Cherry and Early American stains.

3. Basecoat inside the tray with Wrought Iron (although Licorice or Thicket would make a good background for the peaches, also).

4. Transfer the pattern to the tray.

5. Paint the peaches and leaves according to pages 17, 30-31, using the palette above.

6. Basecoat the branch with Nutmeg. Shade with Burnt Umber and highlight with Yellow Ochre and Settler's Blue.

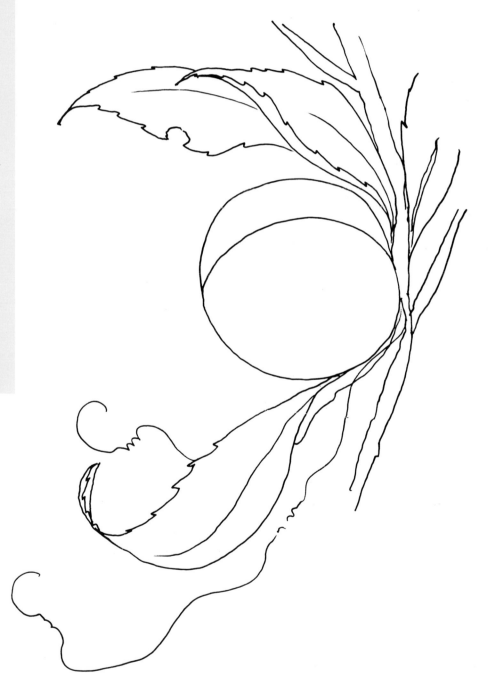

A Pail of Peaches

Surface Source
This wooden cutout with wire handle is available from Oakcreek Woodworks, Rt. 1, Box 1718, Pineville, MO 64856. Phone (800) 477-4434; fax (417) 226-4778.

FolkArt Colors

Peaches
Alizarin Crimson
Burnt Carmine
Buttercup
Clay Bisque
English Mustard
Glazed Carrots
Settler's Blue

Leaves
Clay Bisque
Grass Green
Green Meadow or medium
    green of your choice
Wrought Iron

Pail
Indigo
Slate Blue
Wicker White

Other Supplies
Small natural sponge

1. Prepare the wood piece according to the instructions for wood found on page 13.

2. Transfer the pattern to the wood.

3. The spatterware effect on the pail is done with sponging. First basecoat the pail with Slate Blue. Then, using a small natural sponge, pounce with Indigo. While wet, pounce Wicker White into the Indigo, adding more white to the center of the pail while leaving the sides darker.

4. Float Indigo on the pail to make the bands around the top and center. Add highlights by lightly streaking Wicker White vertically down the center.

5. Add colors from your peach palette here and there into the pail, much as you would tint the leaves.

6. Paint the peaches as directed on page 17 and the leaves as shown on pages 30-31.

Tip
The blue in this spatterware pail and the orange in the peaches have a nice contrast that works well with each other. This color scheme is called *complementary*. Complementary colors are two colors directly opposite each other on the color wheel: orange and blue, red and green, and purple and yellow.

Enlarge pattern on photocopier 142 percent to return to full size.

Delicious Fruit Basket

Surface Source

This project uses the same wooden cutout with wire handle as *A Pail of Peaches* (page 37). It is available from Oakcreek Woodworks, Rt. 1, Box 1718, Pineville, MO 64856. Phone (800) 477-4434; fax (417) 226-4778.

FolkArt Colors

Pears
Alizarin Crimson
Burnt Sienna
Burnt Umber
Clay Bisque
Licorice
Maple Syrup
Settler's Blue
Yellow Ochre

Leaves
Clay Bisque
Grass Green
Green Meadow or medium
  green of your choice
Wrought Iron

Other Supplies
FolkArt Waterbase Antiquing Apple Butter Brown
Extra-fine black permanent marker
Minwax Fruitwood Wood Finish

1. Prepare the wood piece according to instructions on page 13.

2. Stain the basket area with a light brown stain of your choice, such as Fruitwood. Let dry and transfer the pattern of the basket and pears. Transfer a minimum of detail on the basket area.

3. Draw the basket details and shade by lining with an extra-fine point permanent market.

4. Antique the basket area with Apple Butter Brown on both sides, leaving the center clean. This will give the basket a rounded look.

5. Paint the pears as instructed on pages 22–23 and the leaves as shown on pages 30–31.

Enlarge pattern on photocopier 142 percent to return to full size.

Sweet Tooth's Delight

Surface Source
This glass jam jar with a 4-inch diameter (10.2cm) wooden lid is available from Allen's Wood Crafts, 3020 Dogwood Lane, Rt. 3, Sapulpa, OK 74066. Phone (918) 224-8796.

FolkArt Colors

Gooseberries
- Alizarin Crimson
- Burnt Umber
- Butter Pecan
- Clay Bisque
- Clover
- Settler's Blue
- Wrought Iron

Blueberries
- Alizarin Crimson
- Amish Blue
- Clay Bisque
- Indigo
- Settler's Blue
- Slate Blue

Strawberries
- Bayberry
- Calico Red
- Clay Bisque
- Grass Green
- Green Meadow
- Licorice
- Raspberry Wine
- Yellow Ochre

Strokework Border
- Honeycomb

1. Prepare the wood and transfer the pattern according to the instructions on page 13.

2. Basecoat the lid with Wrought Iron. Let dry.

3. Paint the gooseberries, blueberries and strawberries using the palettes above and following general instructions on pages 22-25.

4. Using a liner brush, paint the S-stroke border around the lid with Honeycomb. On the border, use a stylus to add tiny dots of Alizarin Crimson in groups of three.

A Battenburg Lace Trio

(Finished project shown on page 40.)

Supplies
You will need one 10-inch (25.4cm) and two 6-inch (15.2cm) round Battenburg lace doilies to complete this project.

FolkArt Colors

Cherries
Burnt Carmine
Calico Red
Clay Bisque
Grass Green
Green Meadow
Honeycomb
Nutmeg
Raspberry Wine
Settler's Blue
Yellow Ochre

Plums
Alizarin Crimson
Amish Blue
Clay Bisque
Indigo
Settler's Blue
Slate Blue

Pears
Alizarin Crimson
Burnt Sienna
Burnt Umber
Clay Bisque
Licorice
Maple Syrup
Settler's Blue
Wicker White
Yellow Ochre

Leaves
Clay Bisque
Grass Green
Green Meadow or medium
    green of your choice
Wrought Iron

1. Following the instructions for painting on fabric on page 13—mix your acrylic paints with Textile Medium before beginning.

2. Transfer the patterns to the doilies (plum on the large doily and pear and cherries on the smaller doilies).

3. Paint the fruits on the doilies as directed on pages 20–23 and the leaves as shown on pages 30–31, with one exception: this lace is such a sharp white, I added some Wicker White to the highlights of the fruit to brighten them. If the lace had been natural in color, this would have been unnecessary.

Tip
If your highlights look dull or muddy when working on light, bright backgrounds, paint the object as instructed, then add a small amount of Wicker White to the highlights.

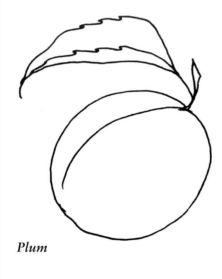

Plum

Pear

Cherries

Tea Time

(Finished project shown on page 44.)

Supplies
Enamelware teapot and cup

FolkArt Colors

Blueberries
Alizarin Crimson
Amish Blue
Clay Bisque
Indigo
Settler's Blue
Slate Blue

Cherries
Burnt Carmine
Calico Red
Clay Bisque
Grass Green
Green Meadow
Honeycomb
Nutmeg
Raspberry Wine
Settler's Blue
Yellow Ochre

Leaves
Clay Bisque
Grass Green
Green Meadow or medium
   green of your choice
Wrought Iron

Teapot
Licorice
Wicker White

There's nothing more interesting to paint on than treasures from flea markets, garage sales and antique shops. This teapot and cup are perfect examples. I bought them separately long ago, waiting for the right time to use them. With the matching border patterns, they go together well. These simple fruits in basic colors add a cozy touch to a country kitchen.

1. Prepare metal according to the instructions on page 13.

2. Transfer the cherry pattern to the teapot and the blueberry pattern to the cup.

3. Paint the cherries and blueberries according to the instructions on pages 20–23 and the leaves as instructed on pages 30–31, using the palettes above.

4. Paint a Licorice band around the top of the cup. Also paint the teapot handle and top of the teapot dome with Licorice.

5. Now paint Wicker White zigzags on the Licorice areas on the cup and teapot using a ¼-inch (.6cm) angle brush. Finish with Licorice zigzags around the bottom of the teapot. A comma stroke or S-stroke border would work well, too.

Cherries

Blueberries

An Apple a Day

Surface Source
This wooden cutout with wire handle is available from Oakcreek Woodworks, Rt. 1, Box 1718, Pineville, MO 64856. Phone (800) 477-4434; fax (417) 226-4778.

FolkArt Colors

Apples
Burnt Carmine
Burnt Umber
Buttercup
Calico Red
Clay Bisque
Raspberry Wine
Settler's Blue

Leaves
Clay Bisque
Grass Green
Green Meadow or medium
   green of your choice
Wrought Iron

Pail
Dark Gray
Gray Flannel
Licorice
Wicker White

1. Prepare the wood piece according to the wood instructions on page 13.

2. Transfer the pattern to the wood.

3. Basecoat the enamelware pail area with Wicker White. While wet, side-load your large flat or angle brush with Dark Gray and blend into the white vertically at the sides of the pail until well blended. Float Dark Gray above and below the band across the center of the pail.

4. Basecoat the top lip of the pail with Licorice. Add a highlight in the center area of the lip with Gray Flannel. Add chips in the enamel with Licorice.

5. Tint the pail here and there with colors from the apple palette.

6. Paint the apples and leaves according to instructions on pages 18–19 and 30–31.

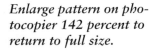

Enlarge pattern on photocopier 142 percent to return to full size.

Scrumptious Scissors Holder

Surface Source
This 8″ × 4½″ × ½″ (20.3cm × 11.4cm × 1.3cm) wooden scissors holder is available from Douglas Malaznik, 14215 Westmore, Livonia, MI 48154. Phone (734) 422-6466.

FolkArt Colors

Strawberries
  Bayberry
  Burnt Carmine
  Calico Red
  Clay Bisque
  Grass Green
  Green Meadow
  Licorice
  Raspberry Wine
  Yellow Ochre

Leaves
  Clay Bisque
  Grass Green
  Green Meadow or medium
    green of your choice
  Wrought Iron

Other Supplies
  Minwax Early American
    Wood Finish

1. Prepare the wood piece according to instructions on page 13.

2. Basecoat the front of the wood piece with Wrought Iron. Let dry.

3. Stain the sides and back with Minwax Early American.

4. Paint the strawberries and leaves according to the instructions on pages 24–25 and 30–31.

Tip
This strawberry design can be adapted to fit many other surfaces by changing the direction of the flowing leaves or eliminating them altogether. I can imagine it on anything from the center front of dresser drawers to potpourri boxes.

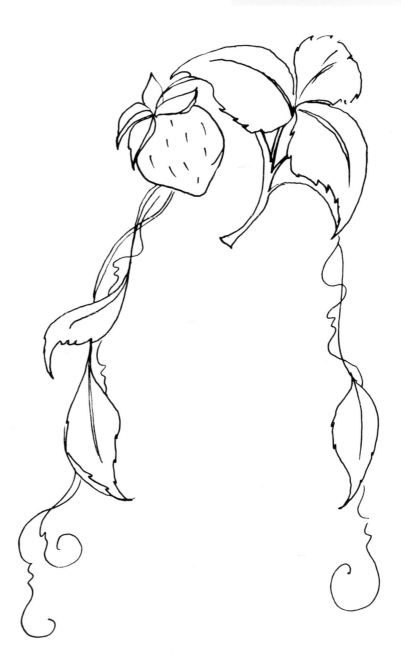

Gourmet's Treasure Chest

Surface Source
This 5¼″ × 3¾″ × 4″ (14cm × 9.5cm × 10.2cm) wooden recipe box is available from Viking Woodcrafts, Inc., 1317 8th St. SE, Waseca, MN 56093. Phone (507) 835-8043. Please request item number 24-1728.

FolkArt Colors

Blackberries
Alizarin Crimson
Clay Bisque
Grass Green
Green Meadow
Settler's Blue
Violet Pansy
Yellow Ochre

Leaves and Branches
Burnt Umber
Clay Bisque
Grass Green
Green Meadow or medium
    green of your choice
Nutmeg
Wrought Iron

Other Supplies
FolkArt Waterbase Antiquing
    Wood 'N' Bucket Brown
Minwax Cherry Wood Finish
Minwax Early American
    Wood Finish

1. Sand the box to remove any rough areas. Wipe with a tack cloth.

2. Stain the box according to the instructions on page 13, using Minwax Cherry and Early American stains. Let dry. Antique by floating Wood 'N' Bucket Brown.

3. Basecoat the background area Wrought Iron.

4. Transfer the pattern to the recipe box.

5. Paint the blackberries and leaves according to the instructions on pages 24-25 and 30-31, using the palettes above.

6. Basecoat the branch with Nutmeg. Shade with Burnt Umber and highlight with Yellow Ochre while still wet. Tint here and there with Grass Green and the berry colors.

7. Paint the lettering by double loading a no. 1 or no. 2 flat brush with Settler's Blue on one side and Violet Pansy on the other. Use the full flat brush for the wide parts of the letters and the chisel edge for the narrow areas.

Blossoms & Berries

EARRING CADDIE AND DRESSER BOX

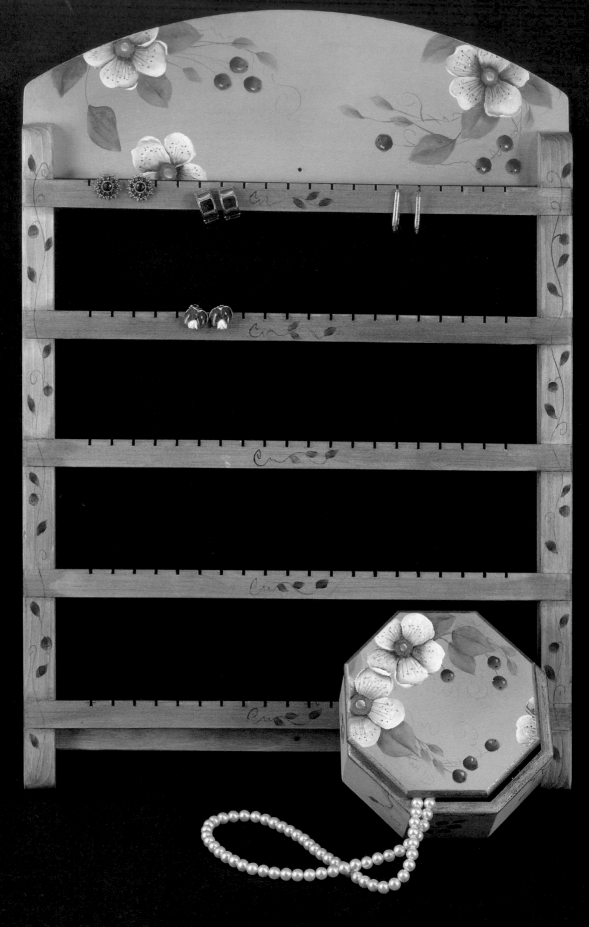

Blossoms & Berries Treasure Set

Surface Source

These three pieces are available separately from Sechtem's Wood Products, 533 Margaret St., Russell, KS 67665. Phone (913) 483-2912, (800) 255-4285. The lidded dresser box, item number 112D, is 5¼″×2″ (13.3cm× 5.1cm) deep. The earring caddie, item number ER-1, is 16″×21″ (40.6cm×53.3cm). The heart-shaped treasure box is 20″×10″×16″ (50.8cm×25.4cm ×40.6cm).

FolkArt Colors

Alizarin Crimson
Burnt Carmine
Burnt Umber
Calico Red
English Mustard
Glazed Carrots
Gray Green
Hauser Green Light
Hauser Green Medium
Nutmeg
Pure Gold Metallic
Southern Pine
Taffy
Warm White
Wicker White
Yellow Light

Other Supplies

Minwax Fruitwood
    Wood Finish
Soft Flock in your choice
    of color

DRESSER BOX

1. Sand and seal if desired. Stain inside lid and bottom of box.

2. Basecoat outside of lid and box with Gray Green, using a large flat brush. Tint-tique with Alizarin Crimson in blossom areas, as directed on page 127.

3. Transfer pattern with light graphite paper. Use a portion for the front of the box.

4. Follow painting instructions on the bottom of page 18. Paint the edges of the front bars with Pure Gold Metallic. Float Burnt Umber to antique if desired. Design your monogram as illustrated on page 55.

5. Varnish everything except the inside of the box. Use a waterbase varnish, matte or satin finish.

6. Choose a color of Soft Flock that's compatible with the design's palette.

Paint the inside of your box with an acrylic paint that matches your flock color, then apply the flock following the directions on the package.

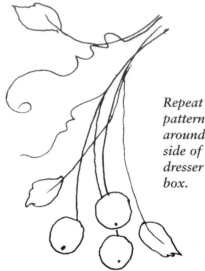

Repeat pattern around side of dresser box.

Pattern for dresser box lid

EARRING CADDIE

1. Sand and stain the bottom with wood stain. Basecoat the top plaque with Gray Green. Tint-tique with Alizarin Crimson in blossom areas, as directed on page 127.

2. Transfer the patterns with light graphite paper.

3. Follow painting instructions on page 18 for the blossoms and berries. The stroke pattern on the stained part is painted with Burnt Umber. Float Burnt Umber to antique if desired.

4. Varnish with waterbase varnish, satin or matte.

(Instructions continued on page 54.)

Pattern for right side of earring caddie

Repeat pattern down side of earring caddie with Burnt Umber. Also use for top trim of wood basket shown on page 56.

Pattern for left side of earring caddie

Repeat pattern for center bars of earring caddie and for sides of six-drawer-chest shown on page 56 (paint with Burnt Umber).

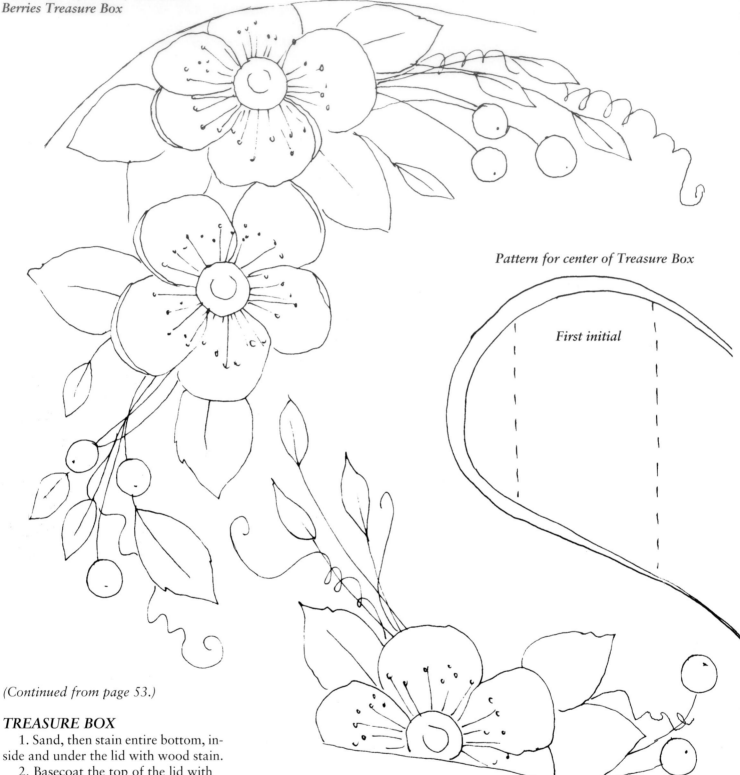

Pattern for left side of Blossom &
Berries Treasure Box

Pattern for center of Treasure Box

First initial

(Continued from page 53.)

TREASURE BOX

1. Sand, then stain entire bottom, inside and under the lid with wood stain.

2. Basecoat the top of the lid with Gray Green, leaving the stained heart shape. Tint-tique with Alizarin Crimson in blossom areas, as directed on page 127.

3. Transfer the patterns with light graphite paper.

4. Paint the blossoms and berries as instructed on page 18. The design on the stained bottom is painted with Burnt Umber. The edges of the top and the letters are Pure Gold Metallic. Line the letters on the left with Burnt Umber using a no. 2 flat. Line them with Warm White on the right using a liner. Antique if desired by floating Burnt Umber.

5. Varnish with waterbase varnish, satin or matte finish.

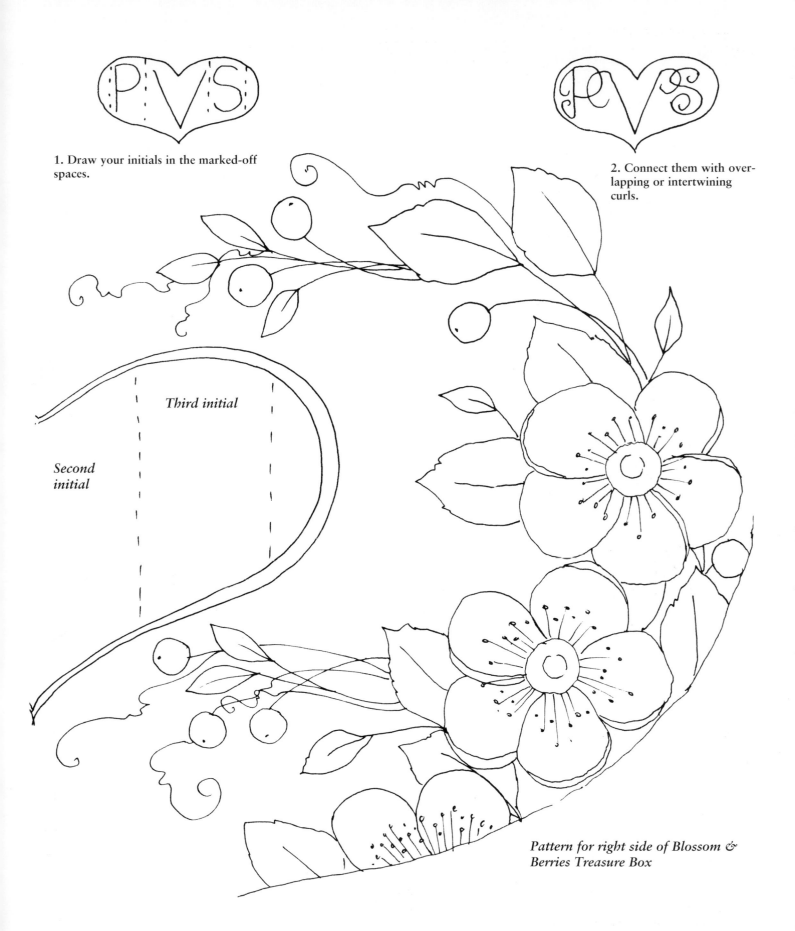

1. Draw your initials in the marked-off spaces.

2. Connect them with overlapping or intertwining curls.

Third initial

Second initial

Pattern for right side of Blossom & Berries Treasure Box

Enlarge pattern on photocopier 111% to return to full size.

"Isn't This the Berries?"

WOOD BASKET AND SIX-DRAWER CABINET

RED CURRANT TISSUE DISPENSER

"Isn't This the Berries?"
TISSUE DISPENSER

"Isn't This the Berries?"

Surface Sources
The wood basket is
10½″ × 6½″ × 11″ (26.7cm ×
16.5cm × 27.9cm) and is available from Woodcrafts, 728 Oak
St., Bicknell, IN 47512; Phone
(812) 735-4829, (800) 733-4820.
The tissue dispenser is 6″ × 14″
× 4″ (15.2cm × 35.6cm ×
10.2cm) and is available from A
Cut Above Woodworks, 9190 Bennett Lake Rd., Fenton, MI
48430; Phone (810) 750-0058.
The six-drawer chest is 9″ ×
11″ × 4″ (22.9cm × 27.9cm
× 10.2cm) and is available from
Douglas Malaznik, 14215
Westmore, Livonia, MI 48154;
Phone (734) 422-6466.

FolkArt Colors
Refer to the palettes for the individual berries on pages
26-29.

Other Supplies
Minwax Fruitwood Wood
Finish
Sandpaper
Fine-point permanent black
pen
Toothbrush for spattering

My grandmother always used this phrase. I'm not sure what it meant
. . . perhaps just a generic phrase for what we term as "cool" now. At any rate, it seemed like a perfect title for these berry sampler pieces. The berries are used together and individually. Hopefully this will inspire you to put a few berries here and there throughout your home. One will certainly add charm to any little spot you might paint it.

TISSUE DISPENSER
(shown on page 57)
1. Transfer the outlines of the background shapes. Stain. When dry, float Burnt Umber around the shapes to antique.
2. Basecoat the shapes with Warm White. If desired, spatter the shapes with thinned Burnt Umber as directed on page 127. Transfer the berry patterns.
3. The berries and leaves were painted as instructed on pages 26-29, except all paints were thinned with water for a transparent effect.
4. The Latin titles are penned, and the background shapes are outlined with pen. Varnish.

SIX-DRAWER CHEST
1. Sand and stain. While wet, float Burnt Umber around the edges to antique. When dry, sand the edges.
2. Basecoat the fronts of the drawers with Indigo.
3. Choose your favorite berry designs to go on the drawers. Transfer with light graphite paper.
4. Paint the berries as instructed on pages 26-29.
5. Transfer the small vine pattern from page 53 to the sides and the strokework heart pattern from page 60 to the top and paint with Burnt Umber. Use the liner brush and the no. 3 round. Varnish.

WOOD BASKET
1. Stain the inside and rim.
2. Basecoat the outside with Wrought Iron.
3. Choose your favorite berry designs and transfer them onto the sides. Refer to the photo for placement or position as desired.
4. The berries and leaves are painted as instructed on pages 26-29.
5. Transfer the vine pattern from page 53 around the rim and paint with Burnt Umber. Varnish.

Pattern for tissue dispenser lid

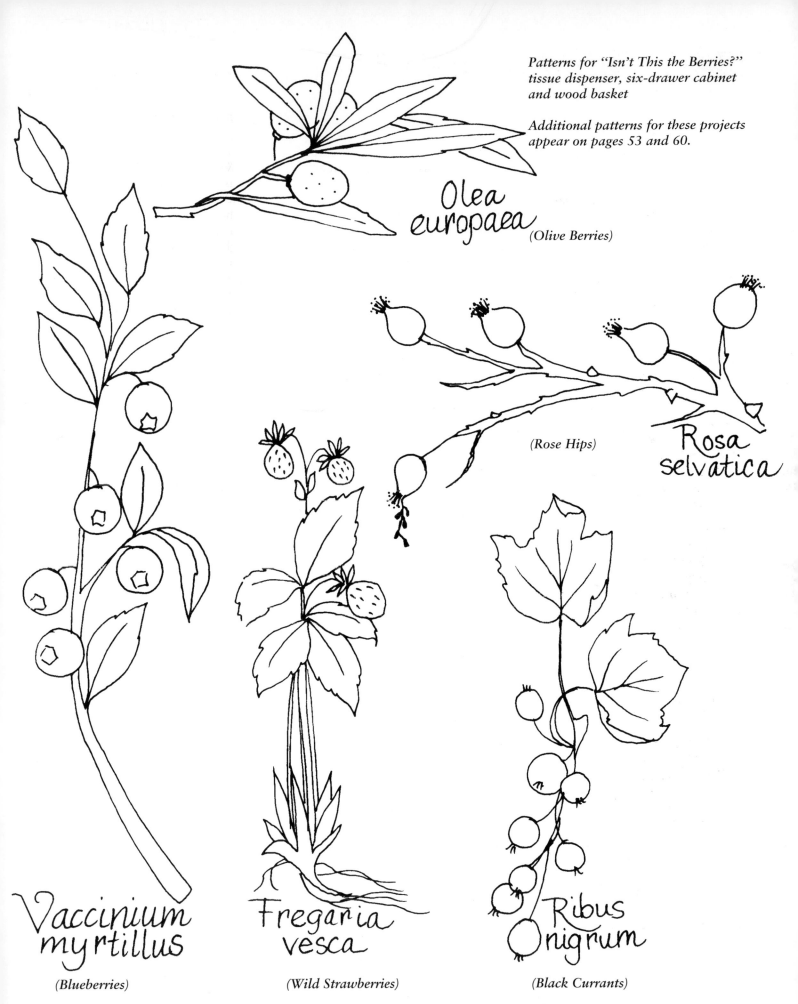

Patterns for "Isn't This the Berries?"
tissue dispenser, six-drawer cabinet
and wood basket

Additional patterns for these projects
appear on pages 53 and 60.

Olea europaea
(Olive Berries)

(Rose Hips)

Rosa selvatica

Vaccinium myrtillus

(Blueberries)

Fregaria vesca

(Wild Strawberries)

Ribus nigrum

(Black Currants)

Red Currant Tissue Dispenser

Surface Source
The 6″ × 6″ × 6½″ (15.2cm × 15.2cm × 16.5cm) tissue dispenser shown on page 56 is available from Hofcraft, PO Box 72, Grand Haven, MI 49417-0072. Phone (616) 847-8989, (800) 828-0359.

FolkArt Colors
Alizarin Crimson
Buttercup
Calico Red
Cinnamon
Clover
Hauser Green Light
Honeycomb
Leaf Green
Pure Orange
Raspberry Wine
Settler's Blue
Southern Pine
Warm White
Wrought Iron

(shown on page 56)

1. Sand and seal the top if desired.
2. Basecoat the top with Wrought Iron.
3. Transfer the pattern with light graphite paper.
4. Paint the berries and leaves according to instructions on pages 26 and 27.
5. Varnish the top with waterbase varnish, satin or matte finish.

Pattern for Red Currant Tissue Dispenser

Pattern for top of "Isn't This the Berries?" six-drawer chest, shown on page 56

The Old Kitchen Coffee Grinder & Crock

The Old Kitchen Coffee Grinder & Crock

Surface Source

This working coffee grinder is 6″×7″×5½″ (15.2cm×17.8cm ×14cm) and is available from Custom Wood by Dallas, 2204 Martha Hulbert Rd., Lapeer, MI 48446. Phone (800) 251-7154. The 2-quart (2l) crock and 6¼-inch-diameter (15.9cm) lid are available from Douglas Malaznik, 14215 Westmore, Livonia, MI 48154. Phone (734) 422-6466.

FolkArt Colors

Burnt Carmine
Burnt Umber
Calico Red
Clover
Glazed Carrots
Hauser Green Light
Licorice
Settler's Blue
Warm White
Wrought Iron

Other Supplies

Sandpaper
Minwax Fruitwood Wood
 Finish
Jo Sonja's All Purpose Sealer
Matte finish spray

CROCK

1. Stain the lid. When dry, float Burnt Umber around the edge. Transfer the pattern with light graphite paper. Sand the edges.

2. Paint the design area of the crock with All Purpose Sealer and let dry according to instructions on the bottle. Transfer the label outline and basecoat with Warm White. Let dry, then transfer the rest of the pattern.

3. The lettering and stroke design on the label is Licorice. Use the no. 2 flat for the lettering, the no. 3 round for the strokes and the liner for the lines.

4. Use the no. 2 liner to line next to the black letters.

5. Float Burnt Umber around the label.

6. Varnish the crock lid. The crock can be sprayed with matte finish spray when dry.

GRINDER

1. Disassemble, then stain the drawer and the grinder's top and bottom. When dry, float Burnt Umber along the edges to antique. When dry, sand the edges.

2. Paint the sides with Licorice. Transfer the pattern.

3. Paint the coffee berries and leaves according to instructions on pages 28 and 29.

4. Paint the stroke design on the grinder drawer and lid in Licorice with a no. 3 round.

5. Float Burnt Umber in the curves of the design to antique.

6. Varnish the grinder before reassembling.

Pattern for coffee crock lid

Pattern for side of coffee grinder
(reverse for opposite side)

Pattern for coffee grinder drawer
(reverse for opposite side)

Pattern for coffee crock label

Pattern for front and back of coffee
grinder

Coffee

Raspberry Muffin Table

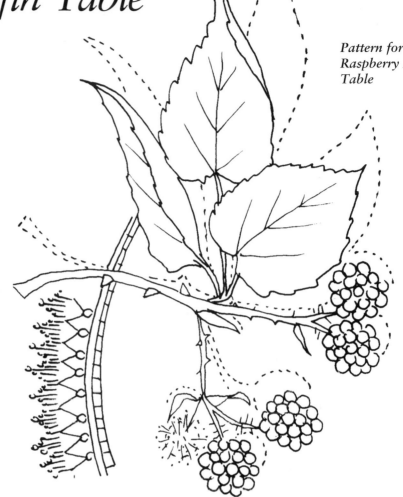

Pattern for top of Raspberry Muffin Table

Surface Source
This 24-inch-tall (61cm) table has a 10½-inch-diameter (26.7cm) top and a 6-inch-diameter (15.2cm) shelf. It is available from Douglas Malaznik, 14215 Westmore, Livonia, MI 48154. Phone (734) 422-6466.

FolkArt Colors

Alizarin Crimson	Ripe Avocado
Burnt Umber	Settler's Blue
Clover	Southern Pine
Dapple Gray	Warm White
Dark Gray	Whipped
Hauser Green	Berry
Light	Wicker White
Honeycomb	Wrought Iron
Light Gray	Yellow Ochre
Raspberry Wine	

Other Supplies
Minwax Fruitwood Wood
    Finish
Toothbrush for spattering

PREPARATION

1. Sand thoroughly. Trace the circles for the doilies on both table surfaces. The top doily is 6½ inches (16.5cm) in diameter and the bottom doily is 4 inches (10.2cm).

2. Stain the table, avoiding the doily areas.

3. When dry, use the large brush to float Burnt Umber around the doily areas and down the edge of the legs.

4. Spatter with thinned Burnt Umber as directed on page 127.

DOILIES

5. Paint in the doilies with Warm White. Let dry, then transfer the designs.

6. Use a no. 2 liner to make a Warm White stripe around the outside of the doily basecoat.

7. Connect the stripe with the inner circle with connector lines about ¼-inch (.6cm) apart.

8. Make brush handle dots on the outside of the stripe, about ¼-inch (.6cm) apart. Space them between the above connector lines.

9. Make V's starting at the dots and connecting to each other (see pattern).

10. Fill the open ends of the Vs with five vertical lines, the center one being the longest and having a dot at the end.

RASPBERRIES AND SPOON

11. Paint the raspberries and leaves as instructed on pages 26-27.

12. Basecoat the spoon with Dapple Gray.

13. Lay the following gray paints out on your palette, starting with the lightest: Wicker White (shine), Light Gray (second highlight), Whipped Berry (first highlight), Dapple Gray (base), Dark Gray (shade), Wrought Iron (deep shade).

14. Sideload to float each of these colors onto the spoon basecoat. Refer to the illustration on page 66 for placement.

15. Add tints of red where you think the berry color would reflect.

SHADOWS

16. Use Honeycomb to paint the shadows on the doily. Use Burnt Umber to paint them on the stained wood. Paint the shadows falling away from the light source.

Tip
If an object is touching the surface on which its shadow falls—in this case, the berries and part of the stem—the shadow is connected to the object. If the object doesn't touch the surface (part of the stems and leaves), the shadow doesn't touch the object. Visualize where shadows would lie.

STROKEWORK

17. Use thinned Burnt Umber and a round sable brush to paint the stroke designs on the legs. Varnish with a waterbase varnish. Wet sand or steel wool between coats.

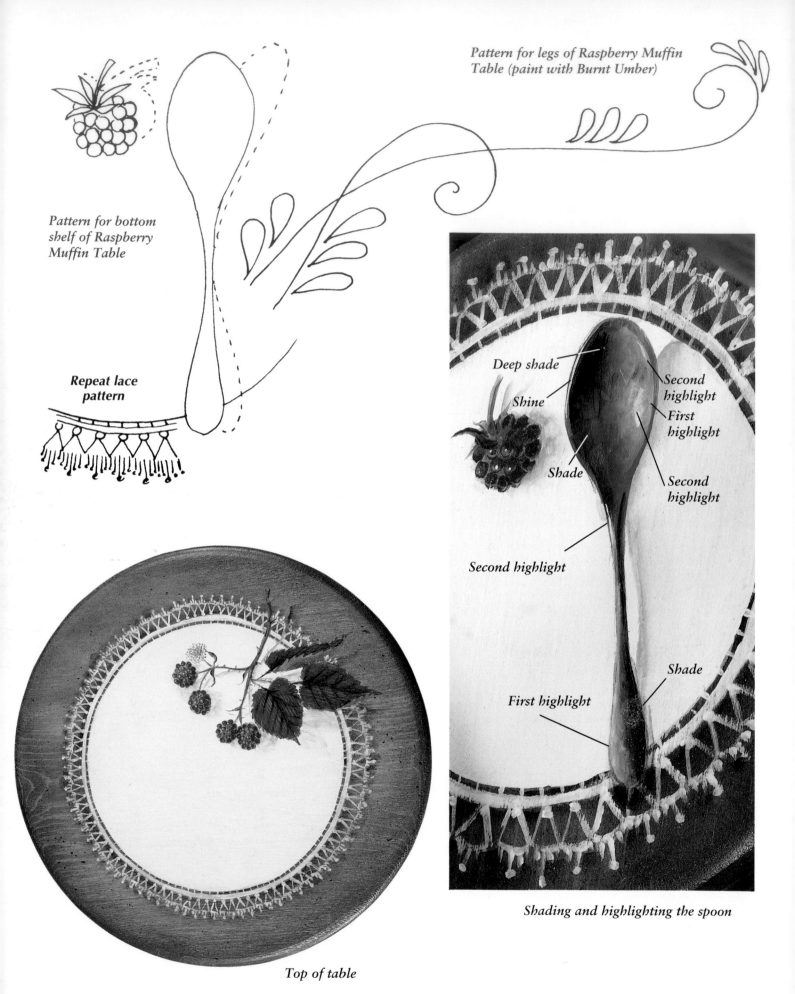

Pattern for legs of Raspberry Muffin Table (paint with Burnt Umber)

Pattern for bottom shelf of Raspberry Muffin Table

Repeat lace pattern

Deep shade

Shine

Shade

Second highlight

First highlight

Second highlight

Second highlight

First highlight

Shade

Shading and highlighting the spoon

Top of table

Nature's Bounty

Nature's Bounty Fruit Bowl Set

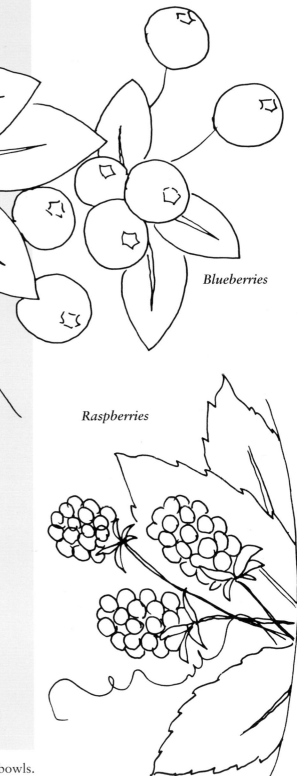

Surface Source

You will need six 5½-inch-diameter (14cm) wooden bowls and one 11-inch-diameter (27.9cm) wooden bowl to complete this project. The bowls shown on pages 67 and 68 are available from Hofcraft, P.O. Box 72, Grand Haven, MI 49417-0072. Phone (616) 847-8989, (800) 828-0359.

FolkArt Colors

Apples
Burnt Carmine
Burnt Umber
Buttercup
Calico Red
Clay Bisque
Raspberry Wine
Settler's Blue

Pears
Alizarin Crimson
Burnt Sienna
Burnt Umber
Clay Bisque
Licorice
Maple Syrup
Settler's Blue
Yellow Ochre

Raspberries
Alizarin Crimson
Buttercup
Clay Bisque
Grass Green
Green Meadow
Raspberry Wine
Settler's Blue
Terra Cotta

Grapes
Autumn Leaves
Burnt Carmine
Burnt Umber
Butter Pecan
Buttercup
Clay Bisque
Clover
Honeycomb
Licorice
Nutmeg
Settler's Blue

Gooseberries
Alizarin Crimson
Burnt Umber
Butter Pecan
Clay Bisque
Ripe Avocado
Settler's Blue
Wrought Iron

Blueberries
Alizarin Crimson
Amish Blue
Clay Bisque
Indigo
Settler's Blue
Slate Blue

Plums
Alizarin Crimson
Amish Blue
Clay Bisque
Indigo
Settler's Blue
Slate Blue

Leaves
Clay Bisque
Grass Green
Green Meadow or medium green of your choice
Wrought Iron

Other Supplies
Minwax Early American Wood Finish

Blueberries

Raspberries

1. Stain the outsides and rims of all bowls with Minwax Early American. Let dry.

2. Basecoat the insides of the bowls with Wrought Iron. Let dry.

3. Transfer the patterns to the bowls.

4. Paint the individual fruit and leaves as directed on pages 17-31, using the palettes above.

(Patterns continued on pages 70-71.)

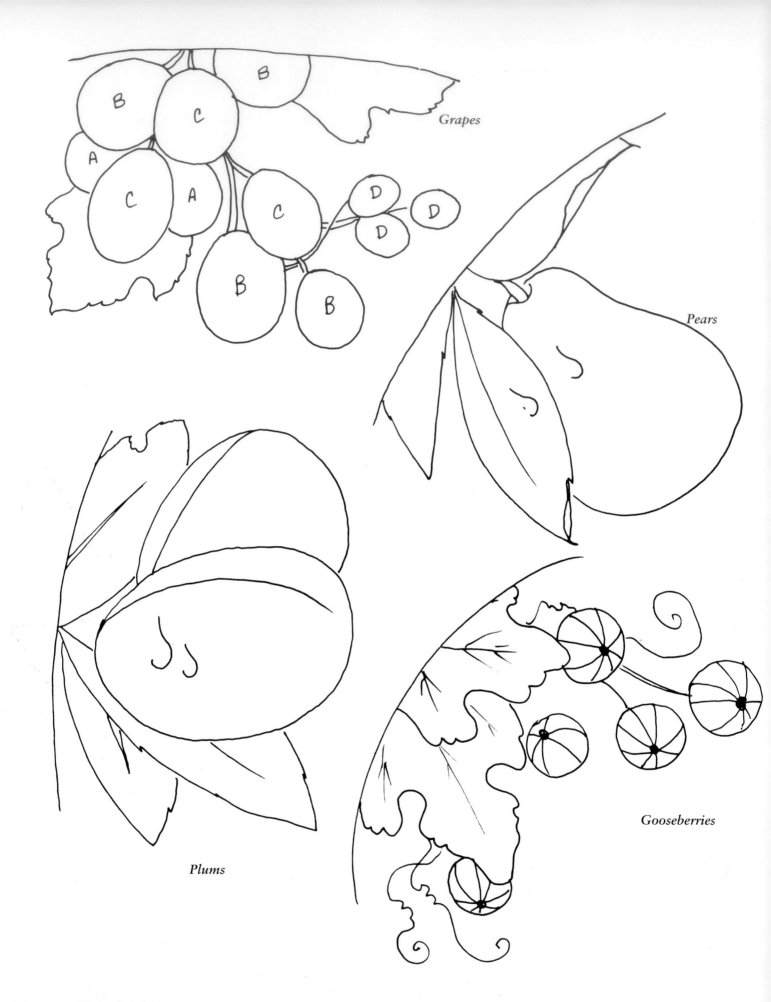

Grapes

Pears

Gooseberries

Plums

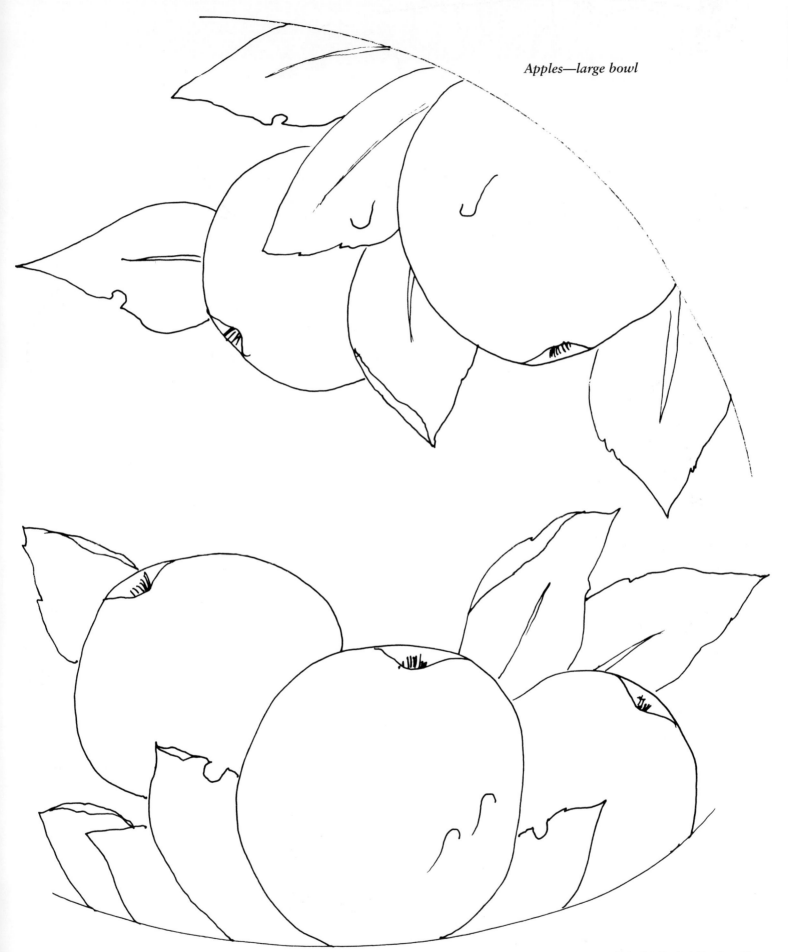

Apples—large bowl

Painting Vegetables

ASPARAGUS

FolkArt Colors
Burnt Carmine
Grass Green
Southern Pine
Warm White

1. Base with Warm White.

2. Wash the top two-thirds with thinned Grass Green. Wash the bottom third with thinned Burnt Carmine.

3. Shade the sides with Southern Pine.

4. The angular buds at the top are painted with Burnt Carmine using a small flat brush. Those at the bottom are Warm White.

CUCUMBER

FolkArt Colors
Aspen Green
Grass Green
Green
Teal Green
Warm White
Whipped Berry
Wintergreen

1. Base the cucumber with Aspen Green. Base the leaf and stem with Grass Green. Shade all with Teal Green.

2. Highlight and paint spots on the cucumber with Green. Shade the leaf and form subtle veins with Wintergreen.

3. Deep shade the cucumber with Wintergreen. Highlight the leaf and cucumber with Warm White. Reflected light is Whipped Berry.

BROCCOLI

FolkArt Colors
Aspen Green
Bayberry
Bluebell
Indigo
Teal
Warm White
Wintergreen

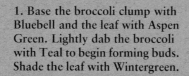

1. Base the broccoli clump with Bluebell and the leaf with Aspen Green. Lightly dab the broccoli with Teal to begin forming buds. Shade the leaf with Wintergreen.

2. Highlight the broccoli with light dabs of Bayberry. Tint the leaf at the ends with Teal.

3. Shade the broccoli with Indigo. The vein in the leaf is Bayberry. Highlight both with Warm White.

RED ONION

FolkArt Colors
Alizarin Crimson
Fuchsia
Tangerine
Warm White
Whipped Berry

1. Base with Fuchsia.

2. Shade with Alizarin Crimson.

3. Highlight with Fuchsia mixed with a touch of Warm White.

4. Stripe with Alizarin Crimson. Highlight with Warm White. Reflected light is Whipped Berry. The inside of the cut onion is Warm White. The stripes are Alizarin Crimson. Tint the lower half by floating Tangerine.

RED TOMATO

FolkArt Colors
Apple Spice
Glazed Carrots
Grass Green
Raspberry Wine
Red Light
Southern Pine
Tangerine
Warm White
Whipped Berry

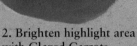

1. Base with Apple Spice. Highlight one side with Red Light.

2. Brighten highlight area with Glazed Carrots.

3. Shade opposite side with Raspberry Wine. The blossom leaves are Grass Green.

4. Highlight with Tangerine, then Warm White. Shade the leaves with Southern Pine, then highlight the tips with Warm White. Reflected light is Whipped Berry.

RADISHES

FolkArt Colors
Calico Red
Glazed Carrots
Green
Raspberry Wine
Southern Pine
Warm White

1. Base with Calico Red and Warm White. The leaves are Green, shaded with Southern Pine.

2. Highlight the red parts of the radishes with Glazed Carrots. Shade the opposite sides with Raspberry Wine. Leaf veins are Southern Pine.

3. Line the radishes with Raspberry Wine. Highlight with Warm White.

CHILI PEPPER

FolkArt Colors
Grass Green
Honeycomb
Raspberry Wine
Red Light
Southern Pine
Tangerine
Warm White

1. Base with Red Light. The stem is Grass Green. Shade with Raspberry Wine.

2. Highlight with Tangerine. The stem is shaded with Southern Pine.

3. Highlight with Warm White. For an inside view of a pepper, paint the center segment with Tangerine. Add seeds with Honeycomb. Highlight with Warm White.

RED PEPPER

FolkArt Colors
Cherry Royal
Grass Green
Raspberry Wine
Red Light
Southern Pine
Tangerine
Warm White
Whipped Berry

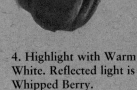

1. Base with Red Light. Shade with Cherry Royal. The stem is Grass Green.

2. Deepen the shading with Raspberry Wine. Shade the stem with Southern Pine.

3. Highlight with Tangerine.

4. Highlight with Warm White. Reflected light is Whipped Berry.

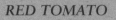

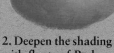

YELLOW TOMATO

FolkArt Colors
Glazed Carrots
Grass Green
Raspberry Wine
Red Light
Southern Pine
Tangerine
Warm White
Whipped Berry

1. Base with Tangerine. Shade by floating Glazed Carrots.

2. Deepen the shading with floats of Red Light.

3. The deepest shade is Raspberry Wine.

4. Highlight with Warm White. Reflected light is Whipped Berry. Leaves are Grass Green shaded with Southern Pine.

1. Base with Glazed Carrots. Stem is Green Meadow.

2. Shade and establish sections with floats of Red Light.

3. Deepen all shading slightly with Alizarin Crimson.

PUMPKIN

FolkArt Colors
Alizarin
    Crimson
Glazed Carrots
Grass Green
Green Meadow
Raspberry Wine
Red Light
Warm White
Whipped Berry
Wrought Iron

4. Deepen the shading at both sides (not the sections) with Raspberry Wine. The stem is shaded with Wrought Iron.

5. Highlight the stem with Grass Green. The highlight on the pumpkin is Warm White. Reflected light is Whipped Berry.

CARROTS

FolkArt Colors
Burgundy
Glazed Carrots
Grass Green
Red Light
Tangerine
Thicket
Warm White

1. Base with Glazed Carrots. Shade across the bottom by floating Red Light. Stems are lines of Grass Green.

2. Deepen the shading with Burgundy. Highlight with Tangerine. Leaves are dabs of Grass Green.

3. Intensify the highlight with Warm White. Shade the leaves by lightly dabbing with Thicket.

4. Add crevices to the carrots with fine lines of Tangerine outlined with Burgundy. Leaves are highlighted with dabs of Warm White.

MUSHROOM

FolkArt Colors
Burnt Umber
Buttercup
Glazed Carrots
Nutmeg
Raw Sienna
Red Light
Tangerine
Warm White
Whipped Berry

1. Base the top with Glazed Carrots. The rest is Buttercup.

2. Shade the top with Red Light. Shade the bottom sections with Raw Sienna.

3. Highlight the top along the edge with Tangerine. Deepen the shading in the bottom sections with Nutmeg.

4. Intensify the highlights with Warm White. Line with thinned Burnt Umber. Add Whipped Berry for a reflected light.

CORN

FolkArt Colors
Burnt Sienna
Buttercup
Grass Green
Green Meadow
Harvest Gold
Lemon Custard
Raw Sienna
Tangerine
Warm White
Wrought Iron

1. Base the corn with Raw Sienna. The leaves are Green Meadow.

2. The side rows of kernels are Harvest Gold (use a liner brush). The center rows are Buttercup. Shade the leaves with Wrought Iron on the right sides. Brighten them on the left sides with Grass Green.

3. Lightly float Burnt Sienna over the side kernels to shade. Add color and brighten the center kernels by dabbing with Tangerine and Lemon Custard. Highlight the center kernels and the leaves with Warm White.

YELLOW ONION

FolkArt Colors
Buckskin Brown
Buttercup
Raw Sienna
Warm White
Whipped Berry

1. Base with Buttercup.

2. Shade and paint the lines in the light part of the onion with Raw Sienna.

3. Deepen the shading at the edge with Buckskin Brown and line the shaded area with the same. Add a stem.

4. The highlight is Warm White. The reflected light is Whipped Berry.

YELLOW SQUASH

FolkArt Colors
Buttercup
Harvest Gold
Raw Sienna
Thicket
Warm White
Whipped Berry
Wrought Iron

1. Base with Buttercup. The stem is Thicket.

2. Shade both sides with floats of Harvest Gold.

3. Deep shade the right side with Raw Sienna. Shade the stem with Wrought Iron.

4. Highlight the squash and the stem with Warm White. The reflected light is Whipped Berry.

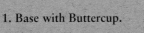

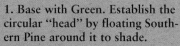

YELLOW BEAN

FolkArt Colors
Grass Green
Green
Lemon
Custard
Southern Pine
Thicket
Warm White
Wrought Iron

1. Base the beans with Lemon Custard. Base the leaves and stems with Thicket.

2. Shade the leaves with Wrought Iron. Shade the beans with Green.

3. Highlight the leaves with Grass Green. Deepen the shading on the beans with Southern Pine. Line the back of the bean with thinned Southern Pine.

4. Paint veins in the leaves and shade the stem with Wrought Iron. Highlight the leaves and bean with Warm White.

PEAS

FolkArt Colors
Basil Green
Grass Green
Green
Southern Pine
Warm White

1. Base the shape with Green. Line with Basil Green to form the pod opening.

2. Paint the peas Grass Green.

3. Shade and paint the areas around the peas with Southern Pine.

4. Highlight with Warm White.

LEEK

FolkArt Colors
Grass Green
Thicket
Warm White
Wrought Iron

1. Base the bottom with Warm White. Float Grass Green into it, then add Grass Green to base the area above the bottom. The leaves are based with Thicket.

2. Shade the Warm White area with Grass Green. Highlight the Thicket leaves with Grass Green.

3. Shade and line the Thicket leaves with Wrought Iron. Use a liner or drag a small rake brush through them. Line the Grass Green areas with Thicket.

LETTUCE

FolkArt Colors
Green
Southern Pine
Warm White
Wrought Iron

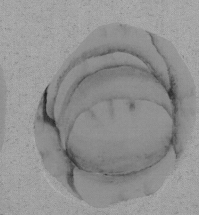

1. Base with Green. Establish the circular "head" by floating Southern Pine around it to shade.

2. Shade with Southern Pine. This will form the enveloping leaves.

3. Deep shade with Wrought Iron. Highlight with Warm White.

KALE

FolkArt Colors
Aspen Green
Light Periwinkle
Red Violet
Warm White

1. Double load a small flat brush with Red Violet and Light Periwinkle. Base with the Red Violet at the edges.

2. Wash with thinned Aspen Green.

3. The vein is Red Violet. Highlight with Warm White at the tips of the leaf.

EGGPLANT

FolkArt Colors
Basil Green
Licorice
Purple Passion
Thicket
Warm White
Whipped Berry
Wrought Iron

1. Base the eggplant with Purple Passion. The leaf and stem are Thicket. The blossom leaves on the eggplant are Basil Green.

2. Shade the leaf with Wrought Iron, the blossom leaves with Thicket and the eggplant with a mix of Purple Passion + Licorice.

3. Veins in the leaf are Basil Green. Highlight with Warm White. Reflected light is Whipped Berry.

BEETS

FolkArt Colors
Alizarin Crimson
Green
Southern Pine
Warm White
Whipped Berry
Wrought Iron

1. Base the beet with Alizarin Crimson and the leaves with Green.

2. Shade the leaves with Southern Pine. Shade the beet with a mix of Alizarin Crimson + Wrought Iron.

3. Highlight the beet with Alizarin Crimson plus a touch of Warm White. Veins in the leaves are Alizarin Crimson.

4. Line the beet with thinned Wrought Iron. Highlight with Warm White. Reflected light is Whipped Berry.

KIDNEY BEANS

FolkArt Colors
Cobalt Blue
Grass Green
Green Meadow
Fuchsia
Raspberry Wine
Southern Pine
Warm White

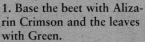

1. Base the outsides of the pods with Green Meadow, the insides with Southern Pine and the beans with Fuchsia.

2. Highlight the outsides of the pods with Grass Green. Highlight across the tops of the beans with a mix of Fuchsia + Warm White. Shade across the bottoms of the beans with Raspberry Wine.

3. Spot the beans with Cobalt Blue. Highlight with Warm White.

BASIC LEAVES

1. Base with medium green. I use Thicket or Green Meadow. Shade by floating a dark green, such as Southern Pine, across the back and through the center vein area.

2. Brighten the leaf with the first highlight of a brighter green. I use Grass Green.

3. Highlight the tip of the leaf with Warm White.

4. Add a stem and veins with the dark green. Tint with color from the surrounding area. The tint on this one is Raspberry Wine.

FLIPPED LEAF

To form a flip, simply shade under it. Highlight the edge of the flip with your brightest highlight color.

BUG HOLES

Add holes in the leaf or at the edge with the background color. Then, carefully highlight the edge in a dot-dash fashion (as opposed to outlining the edge with the highlight color).

PUMPKIN BLOSSOM

Filler flowers are placed strategically to soften the design and enhance the color arrangement. I used vegetable or herb blossoms for the projects in this book. Base with Buttercup, shade with Raw Sienna and highlight with Warm White.

NASTURTIUM

Base with Glazed Carrots. The center of each petal is Calico Red with Buttercup stamens. Highlight with Warm White.

KIDNEY BEAN BLOSSOM

Base with Christmas Red. Shade and define each petal with Raspberry Wine. Fuchsia plus a touch of Warm White is the highlight. Tint with Sunny Yellow.

OREGANO

The blossoms are strokes of Wicker White. Add the leaves after painting the blossoms so they overlap. Use a black pen to add the stamens in each center.

EGGPLANT BLOSSOM

Base with Orchid. Shade at center of each petal with Purple Passion. Highlight with Warm White. The center dots are Lemon Custard.

SAGE

The blossoms are Blue Ribbon shaded with Indigo at the base. The tips are highlighted with Bluebell.

EASY DEWDROPS

1. Float your highlight color to form the drop. Place the drop in the middle-value area, not in the shade area or the highlight area. The float faces the light source.

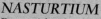

2. Shade under the drop by floating the shade color of the object the drop sits on.

3. With a liner, add strokes of the highlight color in the upper corner, opposite the light side of the drop.

Shaker Seed Lamp

Surface Source
This 8″ × 16″ (20.3cm × 40.6cm) wooden lamp base is available from Allen's Wood Crafts, 3020 Dogwood Lane, Rt. 3, Sapulpa, OK 74066. Phone (918) 224-8796.

FolkArt Colors
- Barn Wood
- Barnyard Red
- Basil Green
- Bayberry
- Burgundy
- Burnt Umber
- Cinnamon
- Dapple Gray
- Glazed Carrots
- Grass green
- Green
- Licorice
- Linen
- Orchid
- Plum Pudding
- Purple Passion
- Red Light
- Southern Pine
- Summer Sky
- Sunny Yellow
- Tangerine
- Teal Green
- Thicket
- Warm White
- Wrought Iron

Other Supplies
- FolkArt Acrylic Antiquing Wood 'N' Bucket Brown
- Fine-point black permanent pen
- Wood stain

Shaker seeds were sold by eastern Shaker colonies throughout the last century. Today there are eight true Shakers left who reside in Maine. This lamp reminds us of an earlier, simpler way of life.

1. Sand the lamp base. Mix Linen with water to whitewash the wood. While wet, lightly antique. Soften with mop brush. When dry, thin some antiquing with water and use a rake brush to lightly stripe, going with the grain of the wood. Spatter with thinned antiquing. All of the antiquing steps are optional. Do one step at a time, study it and decide if you want to proceed with the next or leave it as is.

2. Seal if you like. Transfer the patterns.

DRAWERS

3. The drawer check patterns are painted with a flat brush. Use Plum Pudding on the eggplant drawer, Green on the lettuce drawer, and Glazed Carrots on the carrot drawer.

4. Paint the vegetables and leaves as directed on pages 75, 77 and 78.

5. The "Shaker Seeds" lettering is done with a no. 2 flat brush, using slightly thinned Licorice. Using the liner brush, shadow these letters with Sunny Yellow on the drawers and with Burnt Umber on the sides.

6. The vegetable names and phrase "Quality since 1774" are lettered with the liner; if it's easier for you, use the permanent pen.

LINE WORK

7. The vining and decorative linework on the lamp edges and sides are done with thinned Licorice. Use the no. 2 liner.

LANDSCAPES

8. Base the scenes on the sides as directed on the pattern on page 82.

9. With a flat brush, sideload and pull clouds through the sky using Orchid and Glazed Carrots. Shade across the bottom of the sun by floating Glazed Carrots.

10. Shade across the bottoms of the Orchid hills with Plum Pudding.

11. Shade across the base of the barn's hill and the hills in the foreground with Southern Pine.

12. The barn is Barnyard Red with a Barn Wood roof and a Dapple Gray silo. The doors and windows are Licorice.

13. Use Thicket to pounce in vegetation across the hills. Paint the path Cinnamon.

14. Highlight across the tops of the hills, trees and barn with Sunny Yellow. Line Sunny Yellow on the insides of the framing strokes around the scene.

15. Add more antiquing if desired. Varnish with a waterbase varnish.

Place pattern around top surface of lamp.

Shaker Seeds.

Summer Sky

Sunny Yellow

Orchid

Orchid

Thicket

Teal Green

Bayberry

Teal Green

Reverse pattern for right side.

Bottom edge of lamp side

EGGPLANT

QUALITY since 1774

Basic drawer design

Continue stripe
up the side

CARROTS

Reverse this leg pattern
for other side

(Instructions for Kitchen Note Holder on page 86 and for Counter Top Veggie Scoop on page 87.)

Recipe Book Stand

Surface Source

This wooden recipe book stand is 11½″ × 8″ (29.2cm × 20.3cm) and is available from Wayne's Woodenware, 1913 State Rd. 150, Neenah, WI 54956. Phone (414) 725-7986, (800) 840-1497.

FolkArt Colors

Alizarin Crimson
Buckskin Brown
Burnt Umber
Buttercup
Calico Red
Glazed Carrots
Green
Honeycomb
Raspberry Wine
Raw Sienna
Slate Blue
Southern Pine
Warm White
Whipped Berry
Wrought Iron

Other Supplies

Light acrylic wood stain
FolkArt Acrylic Antiquing
Wood 'N' Bucket Brown

This piece is painted in primary colors—red, yellow and blue—which makes it a *triadic* color scheme. Notice the red is spread throughout the design in tints.

1. Sand the wood and wipe with a tack cloth to remove dust. Draw a pencil line ¾-inch (1.9cm) from the edge of the wood. Using the large flat brush, stain with the acrylic wood stain. Your pencil line should show through this.

2. While wet, sideload with antiquing and float next to the pencil line. Also antique across the top of the front piece.

3. When dry, fill in the background up to the pencil line with Slate Blue. Use the no. 2 liner to paint a Burnt Umber stripe about ⅛-inch (.3cm) in from the outside edge of the wood.

4. To make the S-stroke border on the edge of the Slate Blue area, use a chalk pencil or soapstone to mark off 1-inch (2.5cm) intervals. Paint 1-inch (2.5cm) S's using the no. 2 liner. "Squiggle" between them with a fine line.

5. Transfer the pattern onto the front of the wood. Paint the beets and onions as directed on pages 76 and 78.

6. The rope is basecoated with Honeycomb. Flatten the end of the no. 2 liner to do this. Stripe with thinned Burnt Umber. Use the tip of the liner—if it's easier, a brown permanent pen would work.

7. The lettering is done with the no. 2 flat using Warm White. Shade each letter with Burnt Umber using the liner. Varnish with a waterbase varnish.

Tip

Triadic colors are any three colors located equidistantly from each other on the color wheel.

Beets

Yellow Onions

Kitchen Note Holder

Surface Source
The 21¼″ × 5½″ (54cm × 14cm) three-pocket wooden note holder shown on page 84 is available from Viking Woodcrafts, 1317 8th St. SE, Waseca, MN 56093. Phone (507) 835-8043.

FolkArt Colors
Burgundy
Burnt Sienna
Burnt Umber
Buttercup
Calico Red
Glazed Carrots
Grass Green
Green
Green Meadow
Harvest Gold
Lemon Custard
Pure Metallic Gold
Raspberry Wine
Raw Sienna
Red Light
Southern Pine
Tangerine
Thicket
Warm White
Wrought Iron

Other Supplies
Light wood stain

This is a great project to introduce yourself or your students to painting vegetables. The radishes, carrots and corn on a dark red background make an *analogous* color scheme. Change the color scheme by changing the vegetables and background if you like.

1. Sand the wood, then wipe with a tack cloth to remove dust. Stain with wood stain. Base the front panels of the note holder with Raspberry Wine. Transfer the patterns.

2. Using the no. 2 liner, stripe around the panels with Pure Metallic Gold. Stripe across the top back of the wood with Burnt Umber.

3. Paint the vegetables following the directions on pages 74-78.
Varnish with waterbase varnish.

Tip
Analogous colors are colors located next to or very close to each other on the color wheel, such as red-violet, red, orange and yellow.

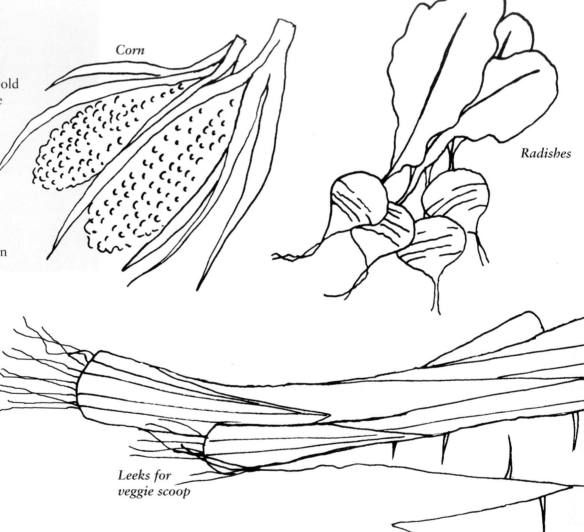

Corn

Radishes

Leeks for veggie scoop

Counter Top Veggie Scoop

Surface Source
This wooden scoop is
6″×21″×5″ (15.2cm×53.3cm
×12.7cm) and is available from
Allen's Wood Crafts, 3020 Dogwood Lane, Rt. 3, Sapulpa, OK
74066. Phone (918) 224-8796.

FolkArt Colors
Burgundy
Burnt Umber
Buttercup
Glazed Carrots
Grass Green
Green
Harvest Gold
Raw Sienna
Red Light
Southern Pine
Tangerine
Thicket
Warm White
Whipped Berry
Wrought Iron

Other Supplies
Light acrylic wood stain
FolkArt Acrylic Antiquing
   Wood 'N' Bucket Brown

I've used this unusual and versatile piece for displaying pretty fall vegetables on my counter, for serving breads and to hold raw vegetables for dip at parties.

1. Sand the wood and wipe with a tack cloth to remove dust. Stain with acrylic wood stain. While wet, sideload with the antiquing and float around the top edge of the scoop, inside and out.

2. Paint a comma-stroke border around the top of the scoop, using a no. 2 liner brush and Burnt Umber. Use the border at the top of page 74 as an example.

3. Transfer the pattern onto the wood. Paint the vegetables as directed on pages 75 and 77.

4. Shade around the vegetables by floating with Burnt Umber.

Varnish with a waterbase varnish.

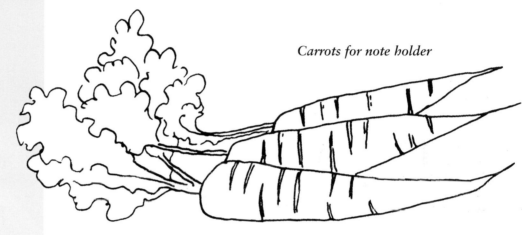

Carrots for note holder

Pattern for veggie scoop

Reverse for other side

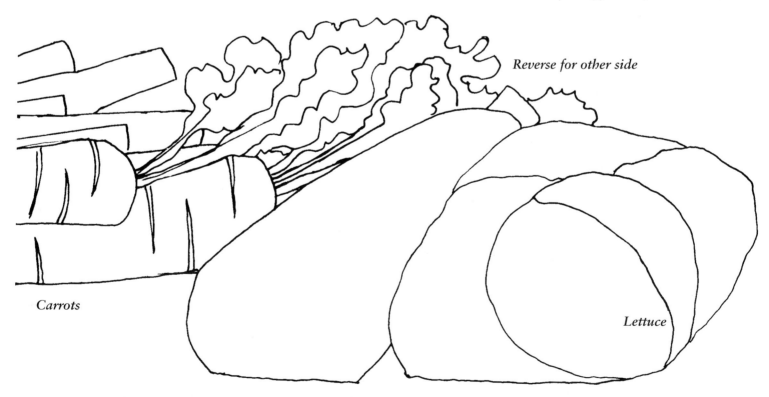

Carrots

Lettuce

Color Wheel Salad Bowls

Surface Source
You will need one 17-inch (43.2cm) wooden bowl and four 7-inch-diameter (17.8cm) bowls to complete this project. They are available from Holland Bowl Mill, P.O. Box 2102, Holland, MI 49422. Phone (616) 396-6513. (The pattern can be reduced if you would like to use smaller bowls.)

FolkArt Colors
Alizarin Crimson
Aspen Green
Basil Green
Bayberry
Bluebell
Buttercup
Calico Red
Glazed Carrots
Grass Green
Green
Harvest Gold
Indigo
Lemon Custard
Licorice
Orchid
Purple Passion
Raspberry Wine
Raw Sienna
Red Light
Southern Pine
Tangerine
Teal
Teal Green
Thicket
Warm White
Whipped Berry
Wintergreen
Wrought Iron

Other Supplies
Light wood stain
FolkArt Acrylic Antiquing
    Wood 'N' Bucket Brown
Wood sealer

Every color on the color wheel is represented in order on the large salad bowl. The small, "filler" vegetables are primary colors—red, yellow and blue. (It was tough coming up with a blue vegetable, but using a little artistic license, broccoli worked just fine.) The largest vegetables are secondary colors from the color wheel.

1. Sand each piece carefully. Stain lightly. When dry, seal with wood sealer. Transfer the pattern. It's rather tricky getting the pattern into a rounded bowl. What I usually do is transfer the main objects first, then fill in. Hand draw areas that don't look quite right or where the pattern won't lie properly.

2. Paint the vegetables, flowers and leaves as described on pages 73-79.

3. Fill in the areas between the vegetables and leaves with stroke leaves of Licorice.

4. Float antiquing around the vegetables and leaves to darken the background around them.

5. When dry, varnish or use Goddard's Bowl Wax to finish.

6. Paint the small bowls the same way. Use the patterns I have drawn for you, or use your own favorite vegetables.

7. To complete the bowls, I painted a small stroke design on the outside of each one with Licorice.

Tip
Primary colors are colors that can't be made by mixing any other colors. Secondary colors are created by mixing any two primary colors: red and yellow make orange, yellow and blue make green, and blue and red make purple.

Enlarge paterns on photocopier 143 percent to return to full size.

Radishes

Lettuce

Patterns continued on pages 90-92

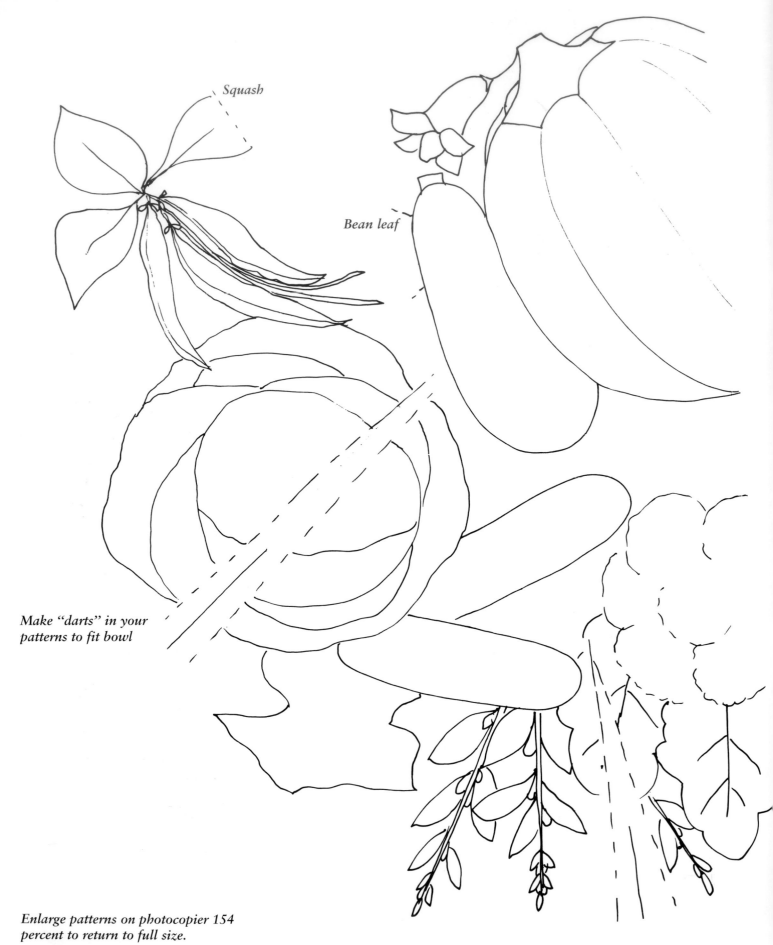

Squash

Bean leaf

Make "darts" in your
patterns to fit bowl

Enlarge patterns on photocopier 154
percent to return to full size.

Dart

Dart

Dart

Eggplant

Broccoli

More patterns for
Color Wheel Salad
Bowls.

Broccoli

Beets

Yellow Beans

Cucumbers

Instructions for Vegetable Serving Plate on page 94, Salsa Jar on page 95 and Kitchen Coffee Service on pages 96-97.

Vegetable Serving Plate

Surface Source
The 12-inch-diameter (30.5cm) wooden plate shown on page 93 is available from Wayne's Woodenware, 1913 State Rd. 150, Neenah, WI 54956. Phone (414) 725-7986, (800) 840-1497.

FolkArt Colors
- Apple Spice
- Aspen Green
- Bayberry
- Bluebell
- Burgundy
- Glazed Carrots
- Grass Green
- Indigo
- Poetry Green
- Raspberry Wine
- Red Light
- Tangerine
- Teal
- Thicket
- Warm White
- Whipped Berry
- Wintergreen

Other Supplies
- Light acrylic wood stain
- FolkArt Acrylic Antiquing Wood 'N' Bucket Brown
- Wood sealer

Tip
A color's split-complementaries are the colors on either side of its direct complement (the color directly across from it on the color wheel). In this project, the direct complement of blue-green is red-orange, so blue-green's split-complementaries are red and orange.

Use this piece for serving vegetables and dip. Enlarge the pattern for a bigger plate and add wooden feet to make it even fancier. The color scheme is split-complementary: blue-green, orange and red.

1. Draw a 6-inch-diameter circle in the center of the plate with a pencil. Draw two stripes around the outside of this circle, one ¾-inch (1.9cm) in from the edge, the other 2 inches (5.1cm) in from the edge. These will form the pattern lines for the light stripe and border design. The lines should be dark enough to show through the wood stain.

2. Stain. While wet, sideload with the antiquing and float around the outside of the center circle. Float antiquing on both sides of the border stripe also.

3. Let dry, then seal the wood. This plate is porous and sealing will keep your paint from "bleeding." Paint the center circle with Wintergreen. Paint the border stripe with Poetry Green.

4. Use a chalk pencil or soapstone to mark off ½-inch (1.3cm) intervals around the circles. Thin Warm White and use the no. 2 liner brush to paint S-strokes.

5. Transfer the vegetable pattern and paint as directed on pages 73-79.

6. Copy the border at the top of page 79 around the outside of the plate. I used Wintergreen, Red Light and Tangerine for my strokes, but you can get creative and use any of the other colors from the palette. Varnish with a water-base varnish.

Tip
To protect your design when using this plate for serving food, I suggest you have a piece of glass cut to fit over the plate.

Salsa Jar

Surface Source
The jar shown on page 93 is approximately 5½″ × 4½″ (14cm × 11.4cm). I bought it at an import store and have seen them at department and discount stores. Any lidded jar about the same size will do. If your jar is clear, paint it black with DecoArt Glossy Paint, following the directions on the bottle.

FolkArt Colors
Alizarin Crimson
Apple Spice
Fuchsia
Glazed Carrots
Green
Grass Green
Ice Blue
Raspberry Wine
Red Light
Southern Pine
Sunny Yellow
Tangerine
Warm White
Whipped Berry
Wrought Iron

Other Supplies
Jo Sonja's All Purpose Sealer

The warm colors in this design bring to mind the flavors from South of the Border!

1. Following the directions on page 13, paint the jar with sealer and cure it.

2. Transfer the pattern outline onto the front of the jar with light graphite paper. Fill it in using a flat brush loaded with Ice Blue. Keep it as smooth as possible. Let dry thoroughly.

3. Transfer the pattern onto the dried Ice Blue area. Bisect the background leaves with Green. Paint the vegetables as directed on pages 73-79.

4. Shade the background leaves by floating Southern Pine at the base of each leaf and where leaves overlap each other. Deepen the shading in the nooks and crannies with Wrought Iron.

5. Highlight the ends of the leaves with Grass Green. Intensify the highlights on the tips with Warm White.

6. The lettering is based in Sunny Yellow with a no. 2 liner. Overlap the basecoats with the following colors: Warm White at the tops of the letters, Glazed Carrots at the center section of each letter and Red Light on the lower part of each letter. Varnish with a waterbase varnish.

Kitchen Coffee Service

Surface Source
The porcelain coffeepot shown on page 93 is 8½″ × 7″ (21.6cm × 17.8cm), the creamer is 5″ × 3¼″ (12.7cm × 8.3cm) and the sugar bowl is 4½″ × 5″ (11.4cm × 12.7cm). All three pieces are available from Porcelain by Marilyn & Lavonne, 3687 W. US 40, Grainfield, IN 46140. Phone (317) 462-5063.

FolkArt Colors
Apple Spice
Alizarin Crimson
Barn Wood
Buckskin Brown
Burgundy
Burnt Carmine
Burnt Umber
Buttercup
Calico Red
Clay Bisque
Dapple Gray
Fuchsia
Glazed Carrots
Grass Green
Green
Lemon Custard
Nutmeg
Raspberry Wine
Raw Sienna
Red Light
Southern Pine
Tangerine
Thicket
Warm White
Whipped Berry
Wrought Iron

Other Supplies
FolkArt Acrylic Antiquing
Apple Butter Brown

The vegetables presented on these pieces are divided by season. The coffeepot has spring vegetables on it, the creamer represents mid-summer and the sugar pot depicts a fall harvest.

1. Sand the porcelain to smooth it. Use fine sandpaper or a kitchen "scrubby." Look at the picture to know where to base the pieces with Wrought Iron and Clay Bisque. Antique the Clay Bisque parts by brushing antiquing on, lightly wiping it off and using a mop brush to soften.

2. Transfer the patterns and paint as directed on pages 73-79. The white onion is based with Warm White. Shade with Barn Wood, then deep shade with Dapple Gray. Line with Dapple Gray. The yellow pepper is based with Tangerine. Use Raw Sienna to shade, Nutmeg to deep shade. Buttercup and Warm White are the highlights.

3. The stroke border design around the lids can be found at the top of page 77. Use Grass Green for the vine and leaves. Double load a small filbert with Apple Spice and Tangerine for the berries. Varnish with a waterbase varnish.

Tip
These pieces can be used for serving. To wash, rinse out and carefully wipe the outside.

Pattern for coffee server

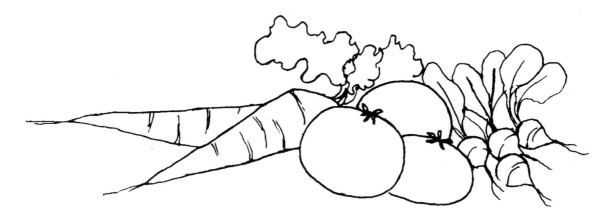

Pattern for creamer

The kiss of the sun for pardon,
The song of the birds for mirth.
One is nearer God's heart in a Garden
Than anywhere else on Earth.

Country Pantry

The realistic vegetables in the center are a nice contrast to the warm crackle finish and old-fashioned strokework and lettering.

1. Sand the wood. Use a tack cloth to wipe off dust. Stain the inside. Base the outside with Apple Spice. Base the door inset with Wrought Iron.

2. Follow the directions on the bottle to paint crackle medium over the dried Apple Spice.

3. When dry, cover the crackle medium with long strokes of Clay Bisque. Let dry.

4. Transfer the patterns.

5. The lettering is done with the no. 2 liner using thinned Licorice. The scrolls are thinned Southern Pine. Use the no. 2 filbert to paint the commas as directed on the pattern. The little stroke radishes are Calico Red.

6. Paint the vegetables and leaves in the center as directed on pages 73-79.

7. Antique around the edges of the cupboard and door by floating antiquing with the large flat brush. When dry, varnish with a waterbase varnish.

Surface Source
This 12½″ × 21″ × 7″ (31.8cm × 53.3cm × 17.8cm) wooden cabinet is available from Douglas Malaznik, 14215 Westmore, Livonia, MI 48154. Phone (734) 422-6466.

FolkArt Colors

Alizarin Crimson	Red Light
Apple Spice	Southern Pine
Aspen Green	Sunny Yellow
Calico Red	Tangerine
Clay Bisque	Teal Green
Glazed Carrots	Thicket
Grass Green	Warm White
Green	Whipped Berry
Lemon Yellow	Wintergreen
Licorice	Wrought Iron
Raspberry Wine	

Other Supplies
Wood stain
FolkArt Crackle Medium
FolkArt Acrylic Antiquing Wood 'N' Bucket Brown

Pattern for door frame. Patterns continued on pages 100-101.

Top of door—reverse for other side

Commas
- Raspberry Wine
- Grass Green
- Thicket
- Calico Red

Thicket lines

Bottom of door—reverse for other side

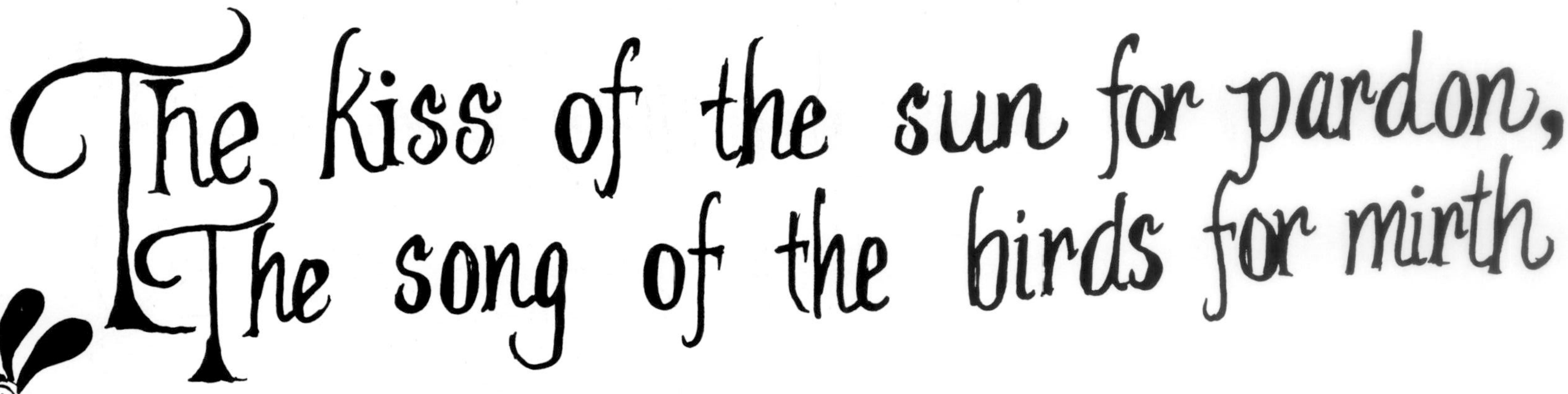

The kiss of the sun for pardon,
The song of the birds for mirth

Enlarge patterns on photocopier 125 percent to return to full size.

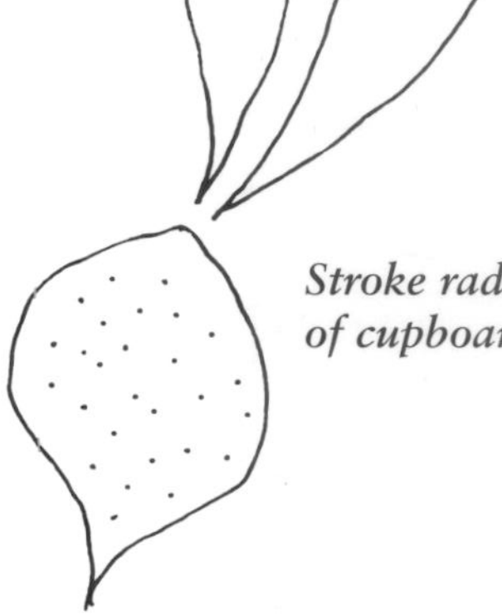

Stroke radish for sides
of cupboard

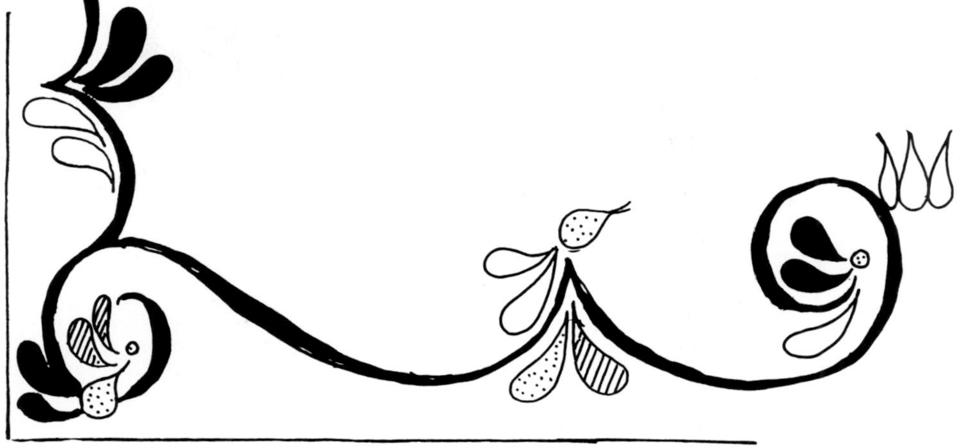

Top of cupboard

Front left leg—reverse for other side

Reverse for other side

One is nearer God's heart in a Garden Than anywhere else on Earth.

Pattern for front of Country Pantry.

Pattern for Country Pantry door inset.

Recipe Clipping Desk

Surface Source
This 10″ × 16″ (25.4cm × 40.6cm) wooden desk is available from Custom Wood by Dallas, 2204 Martha Hulbert, Lapeer, MI 48446. Phone (810) 781-8498, (800) 251-7154.

FolkArt Colors
Barn Wood
Barnyard Red
Basil Green
Bayberry
Burnt Sienna
Burnt Umber
Calico Red
Dapple Gray
Fucshia
Glazed Carrots
Grass Green
Green
Green Meadow
Orchid
Pink
Plum Pudding
Poetry Green
Raspberry Wine
Southern Pine
Summer Sky
Sunny Yellow
Teal Green
Thicket
Warm White
Whipped Berry
Wrought Iron

Other Supplies
Delta Acrylic Fruitwood wood stain mixed in equal parts with water
FolkArt Acrylic Antiquing Wood 'N' Bucket Brown

How many times have you misplaced a great recipe? Use this desk to stash hints, recipe clippings and coupons. The landscape is the focal point, but a vine of pea pods placed in the immediate foreground gives it interest and depth.

1. Stain. While wet, antique by floating the antiquing around the handle and sides of the box. When dry, transfer the pattern from pages 104-105. Basecoat as directed on the pattern.

SKY

2. Make clouds in the sky by sideloading a flat brush with Pink and Orchid and streaking it horizontally through the sky. Float Glazed Carrots at the base of the sun.

HILLS

3. Shade the bases of the Orchid hills by floating Plum Pudding across them.

4. Shade the rest of the hills by floating Southern Pine across the bases.

5. The paths and road are Burnt Sienna shaded with Burnt Umber.

BUILDINGS

6. Shade the barn roof and silo with floats of Dapple Gray. The barn is shaded with Raspberry Wine.

7. Shade the house roof with Raspberry Wine. Shade the sides of the house by floating Barn Wood on the front of the house and under the roof at the side of the house. Float Dapple Gray under the roof line on the front.

8. Make windows using a no. 2 flat brush with Summer Sky. Use Pink with a liner brush to add reflections from the sunrise on the windows.

9. The front door and porch posts are Warm White.

BUSHES AND GARDEN

10. Vegetation in the garden is dabbed in with Green Meadow.

11. The round trees and bushes are highlighted with Basil Green across the tops and shaded with Wrought Iron across the bottoms. Add stylus dots with Calico Red for apples in the apple orchard.

12. The fences are Warm White painted with the no. 2 liner.

PEAS

13. Paint the pea pods and leaves as directed on page 77. The blossom is the same as the kidney bean blossom on page 79, except it is basecoated with Warm White and shaded with Summer Sky. The word "Recipe" at the top is painted with Green Meadow to resemble a stem or vine.

FINISH

14. Highlight all the hills, buildings, fences and plants with floats of Sunny Yellow.

15. Antique the painting with acrylic antiquing. Let dry.

16. Varnish with a waterbase varnish.

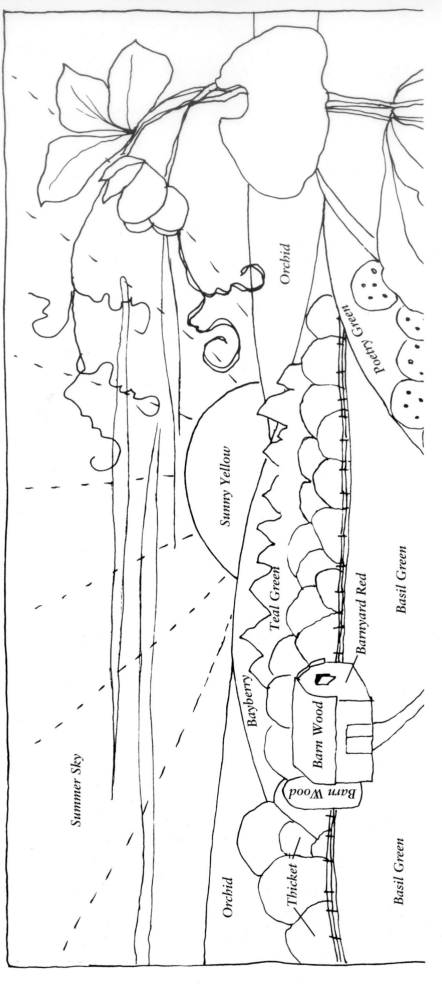

Summer Sky

Sunny Yellow

Orchid

Poetry Green

Basil Green

Bayberry

Teal Green

Barnyard Red

Barn Wood

Barn Wood

Orchid

Thicket

Basil Green

Burnt Umber

Green Meadow

Poetry Green

Bayberry

Bayberry

Barnyard Red

Barn Wood

Warm White

Barnyard Red

Burnt Sienna

Barnyard Red

Bayberry

Poetry Green

Bayberry

wood stain (do not paint)

Instructions for Scarlet Runner Bean Box on pages 108-109.

Left side of wagon

Right side of wagon

Vegetable Market Cart

Surface Source

This wooden cart is 14″×8″×3″ (35.6cm×20.3cm×7.6cm) with 4½-inch-diameter (11.4cm) wheels and is available from Douglas Malaznik, 14215 Westmore, Livonia, MI 48154. Phone (734) 422-6466.

FolkArt Colors

Alizarin Crimson
Apple Spice
Buckskin Brown
Burgundy
Burnt Umber
Buttercup
Glazed Carrots
Grass Green
Green
Harvest Gold
Lemon Custard
Raspberry Wine
Raw Sienna
Red Light
Southern Pine
Tangerine
Thicket
Warm White
Whipped Berry
Wrought Iron

Other Supplies

Delta Acrylic Fruitwood wood stain mixed in equal parts with water
FolkArt Acrylic Antiquing Wood 'N' Bucket Brown

1. Disassemble and sand all parts. Stain. While wet, sideload a large brush with antiquing and float around the bottom of the inside and at the edges of the tongue.

2. The outside of the wagon is based with Raspberry Wine. The top edge is Thicket. I put a decorative stroke border around the inside at the top with Burnt Umber. I used the border shown on page 74, but any other would work as well.

3. Transfer the patterns and paint the vegetables as directed on pages 73-79.

4. Paint the lettering using the no. 2 flat and slightly thinned Warm White. The shadows at each letter and the scrolls below the lettering are Harvest Gold painted with a no. 2 liner.

5. The wheels are striped with Raspberry Wine using the no. 2 flat. Varnish all parts and reassemble.

Wheel

Scarlet Runner Bean Box

Surface Source
The wooden box with handle is 12″×8″×1½″ (30.5cm×20.3cm ×3.8cm) and is available from Douglas Malaznik, 14215 Westmore, Livonia, MI 48154. Phone (734) 422-6466.

FolkArt Colors
Christmas Red
Cobalt Blue
Fuchsia
Grass Green
Green Meadow
Raspberry Wine
Southern Pine
Sunny Yellow
Warm White
Wrought Iron

Other Supplies
Delta Acrylic Fruitwood wood stain mixed in equal parts with water
FolkArt Acrylic Antiquing Wood 'N' Bucket Brown
Fine-point permanent black pen

Scarlet Runners are kidney beans. The flowers are a beautiful red that make for an interesting painting with the red-violet beans. This is another example of an analogous color scheme.

1. Stain the wood. While wet, side-load the large flat with the antiquing and float around the sides, inside and out. Basecoat the bottom with Wrought Iron, then transfer the pattern.

2. Paint the leaves, flowers and beans as directed on pages 73-79. Be creative with flips and bug holes in your leaves as you visualize each leaf.

3. Basecoat the front label with Warm White. Edge it with Wrought Iron using the no. 4 flat.

4. Paint the letters with the no. 2 flat using Christmas Red. Shadow the lettering using the no. 2 liner with Fuchsia. Line each letter with the pen between the Christmas Red base letter and the Fuchsia shadow.

5. The words "Red Kidney Beans" at the bottom are done with pen.

6. On the Wrought Iron edge is an easy stroke pattern. Double load the no. 2 filbert with Fuchsia and a mix of Fuchsia + Warm White for the oval-shaped stroke. The tiny commas between the oval strokes are Grass Green and are painted with the liner brush.

7. Use any color in your palette for the wood handle. I used Raspberry Wine with a bit of Fuchsia at the ends. Sand the edges of the box, then varnish.

Enlarge on photocopier 105 percent to return to full size.

Painting Herbs

Herb Painting Worksheet

(See page 122 for instructions on painting spike leaves.)

"TUCKED" FLOWERS

Sage is a good example of an herb with a "tucked" flower. Peppermint, rosemary and lavender are others. The flower shown here is used in the Herb Pasta Bowl project on page 124. The sage on the Herbarium Cupboard is a slightly different color.

1. Start by shading the base of each flower.

2. Highlight the top half of each flower with the base color + white.

3. Intensify the highlight by floating white across the tops.

BERRIES

These "generic" berries are used in the Herb Harvest Shelf and Herb Lazy Susan projects.

1. Basecoat red berries with Calico Red, bluish berries with Payne's Gray and purple berries with Dioxazine Purple.

2. Shade red berries with Raspberry Wine and bluish berries with Licorice. Don't shade purple berries. Instead, highlight purple berries with Dioxazine Purple + white.

3. Highlight red berries with Glazed Carrots and bluish berries with Payne's Gray + white. Add an intense highlight to purple berries with white.

4. Finish all berries with white highlights and float Whipped Berry along the back edges (opposite the highlights) as reflected light.

"STICK" LEAVES

Dill is a good example of an herb with "stick" leaves.

1. Transfer the basic lines from the pattern.

2. Using a liner brush, paint with Clover. Add more detail.

3. Highlight closest to the light source by lining with Grass Green.

BASIL LEAVES

1. Basecoat basil leaves with Clover.

2. Form the veins by floating Raspberry Wine around them.

3. Highlight the edge by floating white.

Herb Harvest

Surface Source

This 19″ × 11″ (48.3cm × 27.9cm) wooden shelf is available from Custom Wood by Dallas, 2204 Martha Hulbert, Lapeer, MI 48446. Phone (810) 781-8498, (800) 251-7154.

FolkArt Colors

Antique Gold Metallic
Bayberry
Buttercup
Calico Red
Clover
Glazed Carrots
Licorice
Magenta
Pure Orange
Raspberry Wine
Thicket
Wicker White
Wrought Iron

Other Supplies

FolkArt Acrylic Antiquing Wood 'N' Bucket Brown
Minwax Early American wood stain

Growing, drying and using your own herbs is a rich, fulfilling experience—and can add beauty to any room if you plant and dry your herbs on this hand-painted shelf!

1. Sand the wood shelf and wipe with a tack cloth.

2. Stain the shelf with Minwax Early American. Let dry thoroughly.

3. Transfer the pattern with light graphite paper.

LETTERING

4. Using a liner brush, paint the word "Herbs" with Thicket. The letters flow right into the leaf stems. Shadow the letters with Antique Gold Metallic, then outline the gold shadow with a thin Wicker White line.

LEAVES

5. Basecoat the first three leaves on both sides of the lettering with Thicket. Shade at the base of each leaf by floating Wrought Iron. Highlight the edges of the bottom leaf with thinned Wicker White. Make the veins with Wrought Iron using a liner brush.

6. Basecoat the next two leaves on each side with Clover. Shade across the tops of and under the flips with floats of Thicket. Highlight the flipped edge of the top leaf with a float of thinned Wicker White. Add the veins with Thicket.

7. Basecoat the last set of leaves on each side with Bayberry. Shade them by floating Clover across the top and highlight across the bottom with Wicker White. Add veins with lines of Clover.

8. Paint the leaves on the lower half of the shelf as you did in step 6.

ORANGE FLOWERS

9. Basecoat the petals with Glazed Carrots. Float the streaks at the center with Calico Red. Float the sides of the petals with Buttercup and float the ends of the petals with Pure Orange.

10. Highlight the ends of the petals with Wicker White. Add the stamens with fine lines of Licorice.

BERRIES

11. Basecoat the berries with Calico Red. Highlight the upper half of each berry with a float of Glazed Carrots. Shade the lower halves with floats of Raspberry Wine.

12. Add two strokes at the end of each berry on the top half of the piece with Calico Red. Paint tiny Thicket lines coming from the center.

13. Highlight the berries at the bottom across the ends with floats of Wicker White.

14. Add a Wicker White highlight on all berries by lightly "dabbing" the paint on the berry. Refer to the photograph for proper placement.

PINK FLOWERS

15. Paint the stems with Thicket.

16. Using a liner brush, make dots of Magenta, then Magenta + Wicker White, then Wicker White for the tiny petals.

GOLD SCROLLS

17. Fully load a no. 2 liner brush with Antique Gold Metallic. Paint all of the scrolls on the shelf.

18. Shadow the gold scrolls with Wicker White.

FINISHING

19. Sideload a brush with Wood 'N' Bucket Brown antiquing and darken around the curves in the scrolls and the lettering.

20. Antique around the edges of the wood. When dry, sand the edges slightly.

21. Apply varnish and let dry.

Enlarge on photocopier 133 percent to return to full size.

Top corner of Herb Harvest shelf.
Reverse pattern for opposite side.

Herbarium Cupboard

Surface Source
This wooden cupboard is 10" × 17" × 5" (25.4cm × 43.2cm × 12.7cm) and is available from Custom Wood by Dallas, 2204 Martha Hulbert, Lapeer, MI 48446. Phone (810) 781-8498, (800) 251-7154.

FolkArt Colors

Autumn Leaves
Bayberry
Blue Ribbon
Bluebell
Burgundy
Burnt Umber
Buttercream
Calico Red
Clover
Cotton Candy
Grass Green
Honeycomb
Indigo
Lavender
Lemon Custard
Licorice
Plum Pudding
Rose Chiffon
Southern Pine
Taffy
Thicket
Wicker White
Wrought Iron

This piece is faster and easier to paint than it looks. Much of the shading is achieved by varying a single color's intensity by thinning it with water, much as a watercolorist does. The effect has a unique watercolor quality to it. In other places, short strokes with a heavily loaded "spotter" brush are required. The three primary colors (red, yellow, and blue) are used on the front and two secondary colors (purple and orange) are used on the sides.

1. Sand the entire cupboard thoroughly and wipe with a tack cloth.

2. Basecoat the cupboard with Taffy. If you want the wood grain to show through, thin Taffy with water to stain the cupboard. Sand lightly when dry and transfer the patterns to the front and sides.

PRIMULA VERA (COWSLIP)

3. Paint the flowers in two rows using short strokes with a small spotter brush. Paint the outside row Lemon Custard (about five strokes). Paint the inside row with Buttercream (four or five strokes that overlap the top row slightly).

4. Thin Southern Pine with water and basecoat the leaves, stems and buds. Shade by floating unthinned Southern Pine. If the shading needs to be darker, add more layers of floated Southern Pine. Add the leaf veins with the same color using a liner brush.

MENTHA PIPERITA (PEPPERMINT)

5. Use the same method to paint these flowers as you did for the cowslips. First, at the tops of the flowers, use Cotton Candy for the lightest color, then Rose Chiffon for the middle value, and then Burgundy for the deepest color. Unlike the cowslips, these colors should be mixed rather than striped so that the change from lightest to darkest is gradual.

6. Paint the leaves and stems with very thin Grass Green. Shade using floats of Grass Green. Strengthen with floats of Thicket. Add veins with fine lines of Thicket.

7. Add the deepest shading on the leaves and stems with Wrought Iron, but use it sparingly in the darkest shadow areas where the leaves are flipped over. Tint some of the leaves with thinned Burgundy.

SALVIA OFFICINALIS (SAGE)

8. Basecoat the buds with Blue Ribbon. Highlight the tops by floating Wicker White and tint the bases with floats of Lavender.

9. Paint the leaves and stems with thinned Clover. Shade with floats of Thicket.

10. Add the deepest shading with Southern Pine. Use a liner brush and Thicket to paint the veins. Highlight the edges of the leaves where they are flipped over with Wicker White.

LAVENDULA VERA (LAVENDER)

11. Paint these flowers at the top of the cupboard with a spotter brush, first using Bluebell, then gradually changing to Indigo toward the bottom.

12. Paint the leaves with thinned Bayberry. Shade and make veins with Thicket.

CROCUS SATIVAS (SAFFRON)

13. Paint the bulb with thinned Honeycomb, then shade with the same thinned paint, layering the floats where you need it darker. Add the roots with thin lines of Honeycomb.

14. Paint the leaves Bayberry and shade with Thicket. Deepen the shading by floating Southern Pine in the darkest areas.

15. Basecoat the flower with Lavender. Shade each petal individually with Plum Pudding. Highlight with Wicker White. All the shading and highlighting here is done by floating.

16. Paint the center stamen with Lemon Custard using a no. 1 liner brush. Paint the remaining three stamens with Calico Red.

ZANTHOXYLUM (PRICKLY ASH)

17. Paint the stem and thorns with Honeycomb and lightly shade with Burnt Umber.

18. Paint the leaves with thinned Clover. Shade and make veins with Thicket. Deepen the shading under the leaf flips with floats of Southern Pine.

19. Paint the berries Licorice. Highlight them with stylus dots using Wicker White in the upper right corners.

20. Basecoat the berry shells with Autumn Leaves. Shade each with a float of Burgundy. Dot them with Burgundy using a stylus.

(Instructions continued on page 119.)

Herbarium

Mentha piperita
Peppermint

Enlarge on photo-copier 118 percent to return to full size.

Front

Primula
vera
Cowslip

Salvia
officinalis
Sage

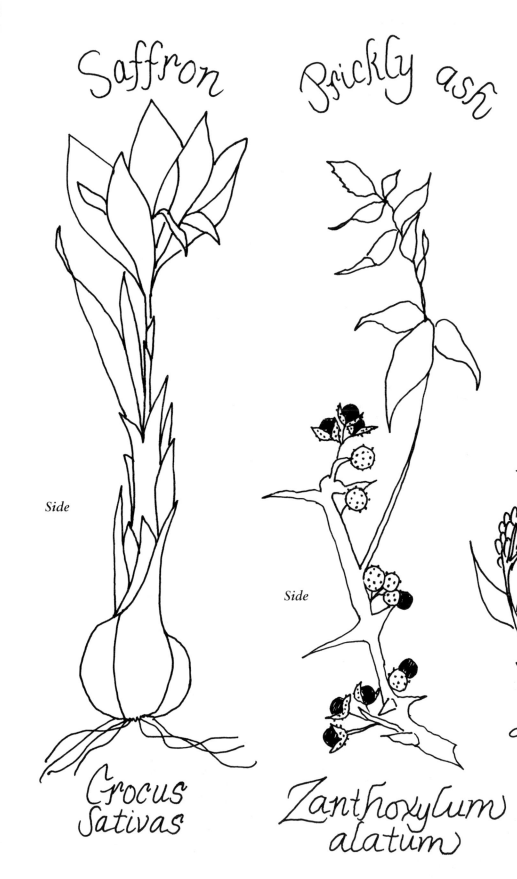

Saffron

Side

Crocus
Sativas

Prickly ash

Side

Zanthoxylum
alatum

Top

Lavendula vera

Lavender

(Continued from page 117.)

LETTERING

21. The lettering can be done with a fine-point permanent black pen or with Licorice paint. If you are using paint, flatten the tip of a liner brush to make it square. Thin the paint with water so that it flows easily from the brush tip. Varying the pressure of the brush when you paint produces thin and thick lines. Experiment with this technique and you will find it a useful tool.

FINISHING

22. When all paint is dry, spatter the entire cupboard with Burnt Umber or Honeycomb, if desired. Let dry.

23. Varnish the cupboard inside and out and let dry.

Herb Lazy Susan

Surface Source
This 15-inch-diameter (38.1cm) wooden lazy Susan is available from Bob Reeves, 11410 Sagegrove, Houston, TX 77089. Phone (281)484-2114.

FolkArt Colors
Blue Ribbon
Clover
Dioxazine Purple
Glazed Carrots
Grass Green
Green
Harvest Gold
Nutmeg
Pink
Raspberry Wine
Sunny Yellow
Taffy
Teddy Bear Brown
Thicket
Whipped Berry
Wicker White
Wrought Iron

Other Supplies
White chalk pencil
Wood stain of your choice

People often use herb wreaths as a decoration in their homes. This herb wreath graces a lazy Susan, the focal point in the center of a table. It is arranged by color to form a simple color wheel, starting with the blue rosemary and ending with purple bay. The design is 14 inches (35.6cm) in diameter and would look great on any round surface, such as a bentwood box.

1. Sand the lazy Susan and wipe with a tack cloth.

2. Stain the wood with a medium wood stain. I used Minwax Early American.

3. Seal the top of the lazy Susan. Let dry, then basecoat with Wrought Iron. Let dry.

4. Transfer the pattern with light graphite paper.

BLUE ROSEMARY

5. Paint the branches with Nutmeg. Line across the tops with Teddy Bear Brown.

6. Using a no. 4 round brush, make the long, narrow leaves with Grass Green. Line the leaves with Thicket, then highlight the ones closest to the center of the lazy Susan with Taffy.

7. Paint the blossoms with Blue Ribbon. Highlight them with floats of Whipped Berry. Paint the stamens with Sunny Yellow lines and add Sunny Yellow dots at the ends.

GREEN RUE

8. Paint the stems and leaves with Clover. Highlight them with Clover + Taffy, then intensify the highlights on the leaves closest to the center of the lazy Susan with floats of Taffy.

9. Basecoat the petals and buds with Grass Green. Highlight across the tops with Sunny Yellow, then intensify the highlights on the petals closest to the light source with Taffy.

10. Paint the centers of the flowers Green. Dot the centers with Green + Taffy. Add stamens with Grass Green.

11. Line the petals and buds with thinned Green.

YELLOW DILL

12. Paint the stems and leaves of the dill with lines of Clover. Line them with Grass Green on the sides closest to the center of the lazy Susan.

13. Paint the flowers with dabs of Harvest Gold, then Sunny Yellow. Highlight with a few dabs of Wicker White.

ORANGE NASTURTIUM

14. Paint the stem Clover and highlight with Grass Green.

15. Basecoat the leaves with Grass Green. Shade and form the veins by floating with Thicket. Deep shade by adding another layer of Thicket floats in the crevices where the veins meet. Highlight the edges of the leaves toward the light source with floats of Taffy.

16. Basecoat the petals and bud with Glazed Carrots. Float the sides of the petals with Sunny Yellow and the ends of the petals with Wicker White.

17. Shade the center of the flower with Raspberry Wine, making the floats come up the petals in streaks. Add the stamens with Sunny Yellow.

(Instructions continued on page 122.)

Tip
This design is painted as if the light source is coming from the center of the lazy Susan. Therefore, all highlights will be more intense on the sides of the flowers and leaves facing the center.

(Continued from page 121.)

PINK BASIL

18. Basecoat the leaves and stems with Clover. Shade and form the veins with floats of Raspberry Wine. Highlight the leaves and stem with Grass Green, then Taffy.

19. Paint the petals with strokes of Pink. Shade at the base of each with a float of Raspberry Wine. Highlight at the tip of each with floats of Wicker White.

PURPLE BAY

20. Basecoat the leaves and stems with Clover. Shade by floating Thicket across the sides, away from the center. Highlight by floating Taffy. Make lines for veins with Grass Green + Wicker White.

21. Basecoat the berries with Dioxazine Purple. Highlight with Dioxazine Purple + Wicker White by floating across the light side of the berries. Make shine marks by "smudging" the berries with Wicker White. Float Whipped Berry across the backs of the berries, opposite the light sides.

22. Using a liner brush, make two Teddy Bear Brown lines at the base of each berry.

23. Tint the leaves around the berries by floating thinned Dioxazine Purple.

FINISHING

24. Using a chalk pencil, mark off ¾-inch (1.9cm) intervals around the outside edge of the Wrought Iron background. Paint in S-strokes using a liner brush. You can use any color from your palette; I used Grass Green. Dot between each S-stroke with Taffy using a stylus.

25. Apply varnish to the lazy Susan and let dry.

Spike Leaves

1. Paint Spike Leaves (rosemary, for example) with Grass Green using a no. 3 round brush. The branch is Nutmeg.

2. Line each leaf with Thicket.

3. Highlight the tips of the leaves closest to the light source with Taffy.

*Enlarge on photocopier 189 percent
to return to full size.*

Pattern for Lazy Susan

Pasta Bowl

Surface Source
This wooden pasta bowl is 10-inches (25.4cm) in diameter (the handle is 8-inches (20.3cm) long) and is available from Weston Bowl Mill, P.O. Box 218, Weston, VT 05161. Phone (802) 824-6219.

FolkArt Colors
Buckskin Brown
Burnt Umber (optional)
Clover
Dioxazine Purple
Harvest Gold
Licorice (optional)
Southern Pine
Sunny Yellow
Thicket
Wicker White

Other Supplies
Minwax Early American Wood Finish and Minwax Cherry Wood finish mixed in equal parts
Fine-line black permanent pen (optional)
FolkArt Acrylic Antiquing Wood 'N' Bucket Brown

What better way to serve pasta than in a hand-painted bowl? This project makes a stunning addition to your dining room or kitchen decor.

1. Sand the wood bowl and wipe with a tack cloth.

2. Stain the outside and handle of the bowl.

3. Stain the inside of the bowl with thinned Wicker White. This might take several coats to get as light as you like it. When dry, sand again lightly.

4. Transfer the pattern to the bowl with graphite paper.

DRIED FENNEL BRANCH

5. Using a liner brush, paint the branch and seeds with Buckskin Brown. Wash over some of the seeds with thinned Thicket.

SAGE

6. Basecoat the leaves and stems of the sage with very thin Thicket. Let dry.

7. Shade the stems and leaves and make shadowy veins with floats of Thicket.

8. Deep shadow with floats of Southern Pine. Tint a few leaves in the shade areas with thin washes of Dioxazine Purple.

SAGE FLOWERS

9. Sideload a flat brush with Dioxazine Purple and place the base of each flower into the leaves.

10. Mix Dioxazine Purple + Wicker White. Sideload a flat brush with this mixture and float in the upper half of each flower.

11. Highlight across the tops of the flowers with a small float of Wicker White.

FENNEL

12. Basecoat the leaves and stems with thinned Clover.

13. Shade with floats of Thicket on the leaves and line the stems with Thicket.

14. Tint the leaves with floats of Sunny Yellow.

FENNEL FLOWERS

15. Dab the flower areas with Harvest Gold using a scruffy brush or a small deer foot brush. Repeat with Sunny Yellow, then Wicker White for highlights.

LETTERING

16. Paint or write the lettering on the bowl. The lettering is easiest done with a fine-line permanent black pen, although you can use a fine liner brush and thinned Licorice if you prefer.

BORDER

17. Using a no. 10 flat brush, stroke in the squares around the rim of the bowl to make a checkerboard pattern using Harvest Gold.

FINISHING

18. Spatter the entire bowl with thinned Burnt Umber, if desired.

19. Antique by floating around the edge with Wood 'N' Bucket Brown Antiquing.

20. When dry, sand the edges, creating a light contrast against the dark antiquing.

21. Apply varnish and let dry.

Sage

Fennel

Finishing

1. Before applying the final finishing steps, reread your pattern to make sure you didn't forget or miss anything. Check to be sure your darks are dark enough and your lights are light enough. Do you need more tints?

2. Are any graphite lines showing? If so, remove them with the kneaded eraser or odorless turp.

3. Sign and date your piece and wipe the surface with a tack cloth.

4. Apply varnish with a good quality, large flat brush. The finish is as important as the painting. I apply two to four coats, lightly sanding between each with ultrafine sandpaper. On large pieces where you're apt to see brush marks showing in the varnish, I often brush on two to three coats, then finish with spray varnish. It's important to use a waterbase varnish because it doesn't yellow.

Antiquing

Antiquing enhances the piece, mellowing the colors and bringing them all together. There are many ways to antique, and slightly different results are achieved with each.

THE ACRYLIC METHOD

The simplest method is to use FolkArt Acrylic Antiquing. It comes in several shades and is waterbased, so cleanup is easy and if you don't like the results, you can wash it off before it dries. Simply sideload a large, flat brush as if you are floating and apply the antiquing as desired. To soften the effect, mop lightly with a large mop brush. For antiqued, stained backgrounds, stain your wood piece with a light acrylic stain, and while wet, float the antiquing into it where you desire the darkening. I used this technique on several pieces in this book.

THE OIL METHOD

This old-fashioned method gives the piece an overall burnished effect. Give your piece two coats of varnish and allow to dry. Mix Norwegian Paint Medium with Burnt Umber oil paint. Stir until smooth and the consistency of slightly thinned acrylic paint. Brush the mixture over the entire piece. Allow to dry for a few minutes or until the shine starts to fade. Using a lint-free rag or towel, lightly wipe out the antiquing, going with the grain of the wood. Use a mop brush to soften. Leave the antiquing darker in the shade areas and wipe the surface clean in the highlight areas. Your focal point should be kept fairly clean. This is oil paint, so there is plenty of time to play with it to get it just right. It will take several days to dry before you can apply your last coats of varnish.

SPOT ANTIQUING

This method is useful for adding shadows or mellowing in specific areas on the finished piece. Try it for shading hills in a landscape or softening the shading of fruit in an arrangement. First varnish the piece with two coats of waterbase varnish. Allow to dry. Using a soft, lint-free cloth, rub Burnt Umber oil paint onto the piece with your cloth-covered finger. Since the piece is varnished, the oil paint is easily wiped off with a clean cloth if you don't care for the effect.

TINT-TIQUING

This is my term for aging a piece with color. Use it on backgrounds that are painted, as opposed to stained. To apply, paint clear water over the area, then float on the desired color. Immediately mop to soften and diffuse the color.

SPATTERING

I often spatter stained and antiqued wood backgrounds with Burnt Umber to further age and mellow the pieces. On a winter piece, spattering makes great snow. Varnish the piece and allow to dry. Thin the paint slightly with water. Dip the bristles of a toothbrush into the paint, then scrape a palette knife over the bristles, scraping the knife toward you so the paint goes away from you. Try a few test splatters on paper before you start on your final piece. Wipe off any unwanted splatters before they dry.

Index